3rd International Workshop on Computational Terminology

(COMPUTERM 2004)

AA005574

Held at COLING 2004

Geneva, Switzerland
29 August 2004

Editors:

S. Ananiadou
P. Zweigenbaum

ISBN: 978-1-63439-678-3

Printed from e-media with permission by:

Curran Associates, Inc.
57 Morehouse Lane
Red Hook, NY 12571

proceedings.com

Some format issues inherent in the e-media version may also appear in this print version.

Printed by Curran Associates, Inc. (2015)

Association for Computational Linguistics
209 N. Eighth Street
Stroudsburg, Pennsylvania 18360

Phone: 1-570-476-8006
Fax: 1-570-476-0860

acl@aclweb.org

Additional copies of this publication are available from:

Curran Associates, Inc.
57 Morehouse Lane
Red Hook, NY 12571 USA
Phone: 845-758-0400
Fax: 845-758-2634
Email: curran@proceedings.com
Web: www.proceedings.com

Coling GENEVA 2004

CompuTerm 2004
3rd International Workshop on Computational Terminology
Proceedings of the Workshop

Edited by

SOPHIA ANANIADOU
&
PIERRE ZWEIGENBAUM

29th August 2004
Geneva, Switzerland

PREFACE

Computational Terminology is becoming an increasingly important aspect in areas such as text mining, information retrieval, information extraction, summarisation, document management systems, question-answering systems, ontology building, etc. In text mining, the acquisition of new knowledge is best captured through terms as they denote new concepts. Terminological information is paramount for knowledge mining from texts for scientific discovery and competitive intelligence. Currently, scientific needs especially in fast growing domains, such as biomedicine, and the overwhelming amount of textual data published daily, demand that terminology is acquired and managed systematically and automatically.

The aim of this third CompuTerm workshop is to bring together Natural Language Processing researchers to discuss recent advances in computational terminology and its impact in many NLP applications. Topics such as term extraction, constructing and updating domain specific dictionaries and thesauri, and systematic terminology management are addressed as they are a necessary component of any NLP system dealing with domain-specific literature.

The topics addressed in this workshop are wide ranging: from term extraction in various languages using different techniques (verb co-occurrence, information theoretic approaches, etc), extracting translation pairs from bilingual corpora based on terminology, to semantic oriented approaches and theoretical aspects of terminology. Terminology structuring is also becoming an important research topic as the detection of semantic relationships between terms finds applications such as the population and update of existing knowledge bases, definition of domain specific templates in Information Extraction, disambiguation of terms, etc. The discovery of synonym terms or term clusters is equally beneficial to many applications in information retrieval, thesaurus generation, information extraction, question-answering ,etc. The integration of different terminological resources is also increasingly important as one has to address term variation between controlled vocabularies, thesauri and textual data. Terminology has to deal with the dynamic nature of terms, their variability, their acquisition from heterogeneous sources, their integration, standardisation and representation. Research and competition tracks on the evaluation of terminological tools still lag behind in terminology in comparison to other NLP areas. With the exception of the NTCIR-1 TMREC, dedicated competition tracks like MUC, TREC, for the evaluation of terminological management systems, term extraction tools, are still missing. Recently, evaluation in specialised areas e.g. named entity recognition in Biomedicine (BioCreative) proved very successful in identifying key problems in terminology such as term variation and ambiguity.

We would like to thank the authors for submitting their research and the members of the Programme Committee for their reviews and useful suggestions to the authors.

Sophia Ananiadou and Pierre Zweigenbaum

EDITORS

Sophia Ananiadou (National Centre for Text Mining, UK)
Pierre Zweigenbaum (AP-HP, INSERM & INaLCO, France)

INVITED SPEAKER

Marie-Claude L'Homme (Université de Montréal, Canada)

ORGANISERS

Sophia Ananiadou (National Centre for Text Mining, UK)
Pierre Zweigenbaum (AP-HP, INSERM & INaLCO, France)

PROGRAM COMMITTEE

WORKSHOP WEBSITE

http://www-new.biomath.jussieu.fr/~pz/computerm2004.html
http://www.cse.salford.ac.uk/TextMining/CompuTerm2004/

WORKSHOP PROGRAM

and Table of Contents

Sunday, August 29

16:00–17:30 **Poster session / demo session**

A Lexico-semantic Approach to the Structuring of Terminology

Marie-Claude L'HOMME
OLST – Université de Montréal
C.P. 6128, succ. Centre-ville
Montréal (Québec), Canada H3C 3J7
Marie-Claude.L'Homme@umontreal.ca
http://www.olst.umontreal.ca

Abstract

This paper discusses a number of implications of using either a conceptual approach or a lexico-semantic approach to terminology structuring, especially for interpreting data supplied by corpora for the purpose of building specialized dictionaries. A simple example, i.e., *program*, will serve as a basis for showing how relationships between terms are captured in both approaches. My aim is to demonstrate that truly conceptual approaches do not allow a flexible integration of terms and relationships between terms and that lexico-semantic approaches are more compatible with data gathered from corpora. I will also discuss some of the implications these approaches have for computational terminology and other corpus-based terminological endeavours.

1 Introduction

Recent literature in terminology circles constantly reminds us that methods and practices have changed drastically due mostly to the extensive use of electronic corpora and computer applications. What might appear as normal and standard in computational circles has had profound consequences for terminologists; this has led many to criticize traditional theoretical principles and some to propose new approaches (Bourigault and Slodzian 1999; Cabré, 2003, among others; see L'Homme et al., 2003 for a review).

One of the issues at the centre of this debate is that of diverging views on the relationship between the term and the abstract entity it is supposed to represent (a "concept" or a "meaning"). Differing views will inevitably lead to very different ways of envisaging terms and methods of structuring them. Some might be compatible with a given application, while others are much more difficult to accommodate.

In this paper, I will try to demonstrate some of the methodological consequences of adopting a conceptual approach or a lexico-semantic approach to terminology structuring. These observations are drawn from my experience in compiling specialized dictionaries using corpora as primary sources and computer applications to exploit them.

Even though the application I am familiar with is very specific and obviously influences my view on the structuring of terms, I believe this topic is also relevant for other terminology-related applications. For example, in computational terminology, there is an increasing interest for structuring extracted terms (articles in Daille et al., 2004 and in Nazarenko and Hamon, 2002, among others). Automatic term structuration is carried out by considering morphological variants (Daille, 2001; Grabar and Zweigenbaum, 2004), performing distributional analysis to build classes of semantically related terms (Nazarenko et al., 2001, among others), or acquiring other types of linguistic units, such as collocations or verbal phrases, from specialized corpora.

These questions will be addressed from a linguistic point of view, but many have been dealt with directly or indirectly by computational terminologists and, in fact, are often raised by their work on specialized corpora. I will also try to demonstrate that the problems dealt with in this paper are by no means a reflection of a tendency often attributed to linguists to make things more complicated than they actually are. I would like to show that they are a reflection of the functioning of terms in running text.

2 Two different approaches to terminology

The conceptual approach I describe is the one advocated by the Vienna School of terminology that has been and is still applied to work carried out by terminologists. The results of its analyses is encoded in term records in term banks or in articles in terminological dictionaries.

The lexico-semantic approach on which my discussion is based is the Explanatory and Combinatorial Lexicology (ECL) (Mel'èuk et al., 1995; Mel'èuk et al. 1984-1999) which is the lexicological component of the Meaning-text Theory (MTT). As will be seen further, ECL provides an apparatus, namely lexical functions (LFs), that can capture a wide variety of semantic relations between lexical units. ECL descriptions are encoded in an Explanatory and Combinatorial Dictionary (ECD) (Mel'èuk et al. 1984-1999).

In order to illustrate the methodological consequences of the two approaches under consideration, I will use a basic term in the field of computing, i.e., *program*. This term was chosen because no one will question its status in computing no matter what his or her view is on terms and terminology.

In addition, like many basic terms, *program* is polysemic, ambiguous in some contexts, and semantically related to several other terms. It will be very useful to show the variety of semantic relationships in which terminological units participate. Finally, *program* does not refer to a concrete object. Hence, its analysis will pose problems different from those raised by terms like *printer* or *computer*.

I will also frequently refer to a corpus from which my observations are derived. This corpus contains over 53 different texts and amounts to 600,000 words. It was compiled by the terminology team within the group *Observatoire de linguistique Sens-Texte* (OLST) in Montreal. Since I am not an expert in computer science, I must rely – like other terminologists – on information provided in a corpus and not on previous knowledge to analyze the meaning of *program* and the other terms to which it is related.

2.1 A conceptual approach to the processing of the term *program*

When considering a unit such a *program*, terminologists who adhere to a conceptual approach will define its place within a conceptual structure. This is done by considering its characteristics (in fact, often by deciding which ones are relevant), and by analyzing classical relationships, such as hyperonymy (or, rather, generic-specific) and meronymy (or whole-part). In order to achieve this, terminologists usually gather information from reliable corpora.

The corpus first informs us that "program" can be subdivided into in one of the following categories; 1. "operating system"; 2. "application software", i.e., "word processor", "spreadsheet", "desktop publishing software", "browser", etc.; and 3. "utility program". It also tells us that there are different types of "programs": 1. "shareware programs", "freeware programs"; "educational programs"; and "commercial programs"; 2. "command-driven programs" and "menu-driven programs".

One possible representation of these relationships has been reproduced in Figure 1. Of course, my interpretation of the data listed above is simplified, since it does not take into account all the relationships that can be inferred from it (e.g., the fact that software programs or educational programs can be menu-driven). Also, part-whole relationships for some of these subdivisions can be identifed (e.g., the fact that programs – classified according to the interface – have parts such as menus, windows, buttons, options, etc.).

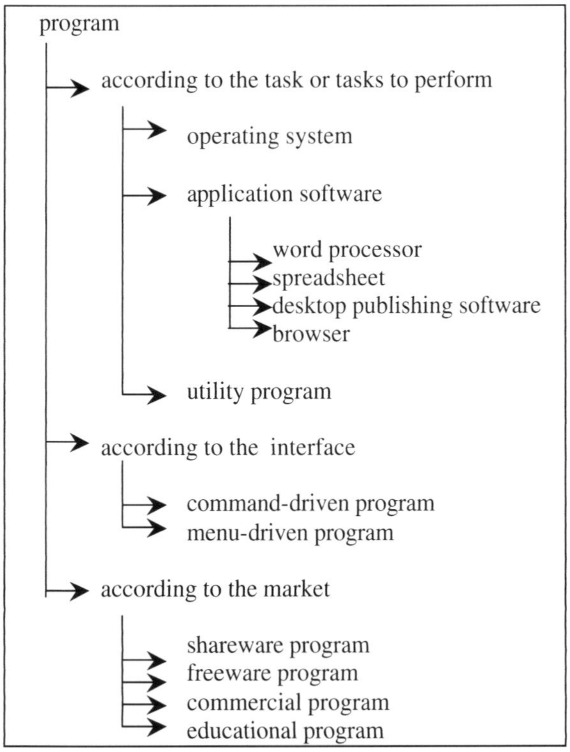

Figure 1: Representation of the relationships between "program" and related concepts

For the time being, I will assume that I have solved the problems related to the relations between "program" and other relevant concepts (which, in fact, is not the case, as we will see below).

The corpus also allows me to observe that the concept I am currently dealing with, has different names: *program* and *software program*. This will normally be dealt with in conceptual representations by taking for granted that all these different linguistic forms refer to the same concept, and thus are true synonyms. In my representation, they will be attached to the same node as "program" (see Figure 2).[1]

Furthermore, since concepts and conceptual representations are considered to be language-independent, their description and representation should be valid for all languages. Hence, my representation system should apply to French (and to true synonyms in French) and other languages (see Figure 2).

program (*program; software program*)
(Fr. *logiciel*)
→ according to the task or tasks to perform
→ application software (*application software; application*)
(Fr. *logiciel d'application; application*)
...

Figure 2: Synonyms in conceptual representations

Regarding this last issue, a choice must often be made between several potential synonyms in order to select a single identifier for a concept. This choice can simply be functional (allowing the labelling of a node in a representation such as that in Figure 1) or result from standardizing efforts. The choice of a unique identifier is central in conceptual analyses, since relationships are defined first and foremost between concepts and are considered to be valid for the linguistic forms that label them.

2.2 Other issues related to the analysis of *program*

In my discussion on the processing of *program,* I deliberately avoided other important issues revealed by the data contained in the corpus. We will look at some of these issues in this section.

First, "programs" can be further classified according to the language used create them ("C programs", "C++ programs", "Java programs"), or according to the hardware device they manage ("BIOS program", "boot program"). Incidentally, in French, the first subdivision (the one represented in section 2.1) corresponds to *logiciel*. The ones we just introduced are named *programme*.

This obviously has consequences for the representation of *program* produced above. The problem can be solved in conceptual approaches by:

a. Considering that *program* refers to a single concept, and trying to account for the different ways of organizing its relationships with other concepts with new conceptual subdivisions. This will produce a very complex, yet possible, graphical representation;

b. Focussing on a single organization of the concept "program" (for example, the one chosen in section 2.1.) and defining the others as being related to vague or improper uses of *program*; or, finally,

c. Saying that *program* is associated with two or three different concepts, and possibly classifying them into three different subfields of computing, i.e., concept1 = micro-computing; concept2 = programming; concept3 = hardware. If the description is carried out in a multilingual context, the subdivision will be necessary to account for the fact that, in French, for instance, *program* can be translated by *logiciel* or *programme*. This latter choice is the one that is closest to the distinctions made with the lexico-semantic approach dealt with in the following section.

Secondly, *program* shares with other lexical units many other different semantic relationships other than the taxonomic and meronymic relations previously considered. All the relationships listed below have been found in the corpus.[2]

- Relationships that involve activities and that are expressed linguistically mostly by collocates of *program*:
  Function: *a program performs tasks*
  Creation: *development, creation of a program, programming*
  Actions that can be carried out on programs: *configuration, installation, running, aborting*, etc.

---

[1]Large-scale ontologies represent concepts and lexical forms using a similar strategy. For example, the Unified Medical Language System (UMLS) (National Library of Medicine, 2004) makes a clear separation between a Semantic Network and a Lexicon.

[2]Some of these have been listed in Sager (1990) who argued that a large variety of conceptual relationships could be found in specialized subject fields.

- Relationships that involve properties and that are also expressed linguistically by collocates of *program*:
  powerful program, user-friendly program; feature of a program
- Argument or circumstantial relationships:
  Agent: *user of a program*; *programmer*
  Instrument: *create a program with a language*
  Location: *install the program on the hard disk, on the computer*
- Other relationships expressed by morphological derivatives terms that include the meaning of *program*;
  programming, programmable, reprogrammable

Most relationships listed above are non-hierarchical and may be expressed by parts of speech other than nouns. Consider, for example, actions that can be performed on a program (*configuration, configure; install; installation*, etc.). [3] Some will be very difficult to account for in terms of conceptual representations. Of course, conceptual-approach advocates might argue that these relationships are not relevant for terminology.

Thirdly, in my discussion of the fact that concepts could have different names, I mentioned only a synonym, but concepts are expressed in a variety of forms in corpora. Many of these will not take the form of nouns.

2.3 A lexico-semantic approach

In this section, I repeat my analysis of *program* this time using a lexico-semantic approach. This approach is also based on data gathered from corpora. The discussion presented in this section is summarized in Table 1.

First, the analysis of *program* in the corpus reveals that it has three different meanings. *Program* can be defined as: 1) a set of instructions written by a programmer in a given programming language in order to solve a problem (this meaning is also conveyed by *computer program*); 2) a set of programs (in sense 1) a user installs and runs on his computer to perform a number of tasks (this meaning being also conveyed by *software program*); and 3) a small set of instructions designed to run a specific piece of hardware.

[3] Another non-hierarchical relationship has received a lot of attention recently, that of cause-effect.

This sense distinction is validated by the fact that *program* can be related to different series of lexical units.

For example, a *program*$_1$ is something that someone, called a *programmer*, *writes, executes, compiles* and *debugs*. It can be *machine-readable* or *human-readable*. It can also *end* or *terminate*. *Program* can be modified by names given to languages, i.e., *C program, C++ program, Java program*. Finally, it can also have parts such as *modules, routines*, and *instructions*.

Program$_1$	
Explanation	Set of instructions written by a programmer in a programming language to solve a specific problem
Collocates	*write ~; compile ~, execute ~; create ~; machine-readable ~; human-readable ~; ~ ends, ~ terminates, debug ~; powerful ~*
Hyponyms	*C ~, C++ ~, Java ~*
Other related terms	*to program; programming, programmer; routine, instruction; module; page; segment; language; line*
Program$_2$	
Explanation	Set of programs$_1$ installed and run on the computer by a user to perform a specific task or a set of related tasks.
Hyponyms	*operating system; application software; word processor, spreadsheet*
Collocates	*active ~, running of ~; download ~; develop ~; run ~, install ~; uninstall ~; add/remove ~; user-friendly; quit ~; exit ~; load ~; launch ~*
Other related terms	*user, hard disk;* *application* *software*
Program$_3$	
Explanation	Short set of specific instructions designed to run a hardware device
Other related terms	*boot, BIOS, to program, reprogram, programmable, reprogrammable, programming*

Table 1: Semantic distinctions for *program*

A *program*$_2$ is something a *user installs* on his computer, *loads* into the memory, *runs*, and sometimes *uninstalls*. Different sorts of programs can be identified, such as operating systems, applications, and utilities. Programs can have parts such as windows, menus, options, etc. Finally, a *program*$_2$ can be *user-friendly*.

A *program*$_3$ consists of a few code lines written in order to specify the behaviour of a specific hardware device, such as a memory. The device is then said to be *programmable* and/or *reprogrammable*. It can be *programmed* and *reprogrammed*.

In this lexico-semantic approach, the relationships observed between *program* and other terms are attached to its specific meanings. This distinction allows us to relate other terms to specific senses. For example, *program*$_1$ is related to other senses as follows:

Synonym: *computer ~*
Types of programs: C ~, Java ~
Parts of programs: *instruction, page, segment, line, routine*
Creation of a program: *write ~, create ~, to program, programming*
Agent: *programmer*
Cause a program to function: *execute ~*
The program stops functioning: ~ ends, ~ terminates
etc.

Since most semantic relationships are non-hierarchical, they can be represented in a relational model. In ECL, paradigmatic and syntagmatic semantic relations are represented by means of a single formalism, i.e., lexical functions (LFs). LFs are used to capture abstract and general senses that remain valid for a large number of lexical units. The relationships listed above could be formalized as follows:[4]

synonym: **Syn**(program$_1$) = computer ~

agent of a program: **S$_1$**(program$_1$) = programmer

create a program: **CausFunc$_0$**(program$_1$) = create [DET ~], write [DET ~]

Cause a program to function: **CausFact$_0$**(program1) = execute [DET ~]

The program stops functioning: **FinFact$_0$**(program$_1$) = [DET ~] ends, [DET ~] terminates

[4]Meronymic and hyperonymic relationships can also can also be captured by means of lexical functions. Authors have proposed LFs especially designed to represent these relations (**Spec,** for hyponymy; and **Part**; for meronymy). However, ECL will prefer accounting for these relationships with non-standard lexical functions in order to explain the specific nature of the relationships between a lexical unit and its meronym.

3 General comments on the analyses of terms

These two brief analyses of *program* reveal the following about terms:

- Terms can convey multiple meanings. This is not an accidental property that only affects *program*. Numerous examples can be found in corpora and have been dealt with in recent literature. This, of course, has important consequences for both conceptual and lexico-semantic approaches.
- Terms can enter into a large variety of relationships with other terms, and not only taxonomic or meronymic relationships. The understanding of these relationships is necessary to capture sense distinctions; in addition, relationships are valid for a specific meaning.
- Some of the relationships observed between terms are hierarchical: hyperonymy and meronymy.
- Most semantic relationships are non-hierarchical: e.g., actions carried out by terms, properties, cause-effect.
- Some relationships involve lexical units other than nouns: e.g., actions and creation are often expressed linguistically by means of verbs; properties are expressed by adjectives.
- Most relationships involve terms considered as linguistics units rather than labels for concepts: e.g., morphological derivatives.

In fact, what these observations tend to show is that terms behave like other lexical units and must be dealt with accordingly. Terms will acquire their specificity through a given application with set objectives, but as units occurring in corpora, terms cannot be differentiated from other lexical units.

4 Implications for computational terminology and other corpus-based work

The previous discussion has a number of implications for computational terminology (as well as other corpus-based terminology-related applications). I will examine a few in this section.

First, both approaches will focus on different types of units when selecting terms in corpora. In conceptual approaches, a selection is made among linguistic units that can refer to a concept. The focus is on nouns and noun phrases. Even though concepts can be expressed in a variety of lnguistic forms, synonyms considered will invariably be nouns of noun phrases. Work on terminological variation (Daille, 2003; Jacquemin, 2001) has shown the variety of forms that terms can take in corpora (morphological derivation, insertion, elision, anaphora, etc.), but these are taken into account only if they can be associated with an admitted term.

In a lexico-semantic approach as that presented in section 2.3, units considered will be those that convey a meaning that can be related to the field of computing (the subject field is delimited prior to the selection). Lexical units selected can pertain to different parts of speech as long as their meaning can be related to the field under examination: nouns (*program, byte*); verbs (*debug, to program*), adjectives (*user-friendly, programmable*). Even adverbs can convey a specialized meaning (e.g., *digitally, dynamically*).

Secondly, any terminological work based on corpora will run into polysemy, even though it focuses on a small set of terms. The manner in which the distinctions between senses are made has important consequences on way terms will be processed afterwards.

Polysemy can be dealt with using a conceptual approach, which considers this property to be an accidental problem. Hence, distinctions depend on decisions made during the classification process or the construction of conceptual representations.

In lexico-semantic approaches, polysemy is viewed as a natural property of lexical units. Senses are delimited prior to the representation of semantic relationships and this delimitation is based on the observations of interactions between the term under examination and other lexical units. Sense delimitation and distinction is a necessary step before anything else can be done.

Thirdly, regarding terminology structuring, conceptual methods, such as the one discussed in section 2.1, are useful as far as classification is concerned. Hence, they can be used for describing concepts that correspond to entities (concrete objects, substances, artefacts, animates, etc.). Moreover, the focus is on hierarchical relations (hyperonymy and meronymy) which is again valid for entities, and, as far as part-whole relations are concerned, more specifically concrete objects. Many non-hierarchical relationships, such as those listed in section 2.3 are disregarded, either because they involve units that do not refer to entities, or because they are relationships between lexical units and not concepts.

Also, relationships between synonyms are considered from the point of view of true synonymy. Choosing a unique linguistic identifier for a concept and considering competing linguistic forms as true synonyms has implications for the variety of relationships that can be considered. Some relationships can be valid for one synonym but not for another.

In lexico-semantic approaches, semantic relationships are attached to senses that have been distinguished previously. In addition, a wide variety of semantic relationships can be taken into account. These relationships can apply to terms that designate entities, as well as activities, and properties. Hypernymy and meronymy represent only a small part of the semantic relationships terms can share with other terms. Other relationships, such as argument relations, entity-activity relations, can be expressed by different parts of speech.

Fourthly, conceptual approaches lead to representations that distance themselves from data collected in corpora. Many decisions are made during the construction of the representation. On the one hand, many meanings that would appear to be relevant in other approaches are not considered. On the other hand, things are added in order to build the representation. Consider, for example, Figure 1. Some subdivisions are created but do not correspond to lexical units (e.g., *according to the interface*); this sort of classification of units will result in considering several complex sequences that have a compositional meaning (hence, that are not true lexical units).

Terminology structuring in conceptual approaches is often carried out in order to represent knowledge and not linguistic units. Problems arise when this work is done using corpora as a starting point, since linguistic units (such as terms) do not behave in a way that reflects perfectly a given knowledge structure. When analyzing terms, considerations regarding knowledge structure will constantly interfere with factors related to the behaviour of linguistic units in text.

On the other hand, lexico-semantic approaches are much more compatible with data gathered from corpora. Of course, terminologists will make decisions since they must interpret data and synthesize their findings, but these are based on the observation of interactions between lexical units that appear in corpora.

5 Concluding remarks

The point in my discussion, is not to say that an approach is much better than the other for terminology, regardless of the application at hand. This topic has been dealt with extensively by authors and even placed in a theoretical perspective. Rather, I wanted to demonstrate that an approach is probably better suited that the other as far as terms considered in corpora are concerned. I also wanted to point out the methodological consequences of choosing an approach over another.

Conceptual approaches will account for consensual representations of knowledge, based on a predefined set of hierarchical relationships. However, in must be kept in mind that resulting representations distance themselves from corpus data and necessitate a lot of hand-crafted changes. Often, the ideal knowledge structure is formulated beforehand entirely or partly, and the difficulty consists in trying to find lexical units that fit into it.

Lexico-semantic approaches will provide terminologists with a framework for interpreting data related to terms and the contexts in which they appear. However, one must accept, when using this kind of approach, that terminological structures are discovered gradually through semantic relations and that some of these relations will even contradict assumed knowledge structures.

6 Acknowledgements

I would like to thank Elizabeth Marshman for her comments on a preliminary version of this article.

References

D. Bourigault and M. Slodzian. 1999. Pour une terminologie textuelle. *Terminologies nouvelles*, 19:29-32.

M.T. Cabré. 2003. Theories of Terminology. Their Description, Prescription and Explanation. *Terminology* 9(2):163-199.

A. Condamines. 1995. "Terminology. New needs, new perspectives." *Terminology* 2(2): 219-238.

D.A. Cruse. 1986. *Lexical Semantics*, Cambridge: Cambridge University Press.

B. Daille. 2002. Qualitative term extraction. In D. Bourigault, C. Jacquemin and M.C. L'Homme (eds.), *Recent Advances in Computational Terminology*, 149-166, Amsterdam / Philadelphia: John Benjamins.

B. Daille. 2003. Terminology Mining. In M.T. Pazienza (ed.), *Information Extraction in the Web Era*, Lectures Notes in Artificial Intelligence. 29-44. Springer.

B. Daille, K. Kageura, H. Nakagawa and L.-F. Chien (eds.). 2004. *Recent Trends in Computational Terminology. Special Issue of Terminology*, 10(1).

N. Grabar and P. Zweigenbaum. 2004, forthcoming. Lexically-based terminology structuring. *Terminology,* 10(1).

Jacquemin. C. 2001. *Spotting and Discovering Terms through Natural Language Processing Techniques*, Cambridge: MIT Press.

M.C. L'Homme, U. Heid and J.C. Sager. 2003. Terminology during the past decade (1994-2004). An Editorial Statement. *Terminology*, 9(2):151-161.

I. Mel'èuk, A. Clas and A. Polguère. 1995. *Introduction à la lexicologie explicative et combinatoire*, Louvain-la-Neuve (Belgique): Duculot.

I. Mel'èuk et al. 1984-1999. *Dictionnaire explicatif et combinatoire du français contemporain. Recherches lexico-sémantiques I-IV*, Montréal : Les Presses de l'Université de Montréal.

National Library of Medicine. 2004. UMLS Knowledge Sources (http://www.nlm.nih.gov/research/umls/)

A. Nazarenko and T. Hamon. (eds.). 2002. *Structuration de terminologie. Special issue of Traitement automatique des langues. TAL*, 43(1).

A. Nazarenko, P. Zweigenbaum, B. Habert and J. Bouaud. 2001. Corpus-based extension of a terminological semantic lexicon. In D. Bourigault, C. Jacquemin and M.C. L'Homme (eds.), *Recent Advances in Computational Terminology*, 327-351, Amsterdam / Philadelphia: John Benjamins.

J.C. Sager. 1990. *A Practical Course in Terminology Processing*. Amsterdam / Philadelphia: John Benjamins.

E. Wüster. 2004, forthcoming. The structure of the linguistic world of concepts and its representation in dictionaries [translated by J.C. Sager]. *Terminology*, 10(2).

Metalinguistic Information Extraction for Terminology

Carlos Rodríguez Penagos
Language Engineering Group, Engineering Institute
UNAM, Ciudad Universitaria A.P. 70-472
Coyoacán 04510 Mexico City, México
CRodriguezP@iingen.unam.mx

Abstract

This paper describes and evaluates the Metalinguistic Operation Processor (MOP) system for automatic compilation of metalinguistic information from technical and scientific documents. This system is designed to extract non-standard terminological resources that we have called Metalinguistic Information Databases (or MIDs), in order to help update changing glossaries, knowledge bases and ontologies, as well as to reflect the metastable dynamics of special-domain knowledge.

1 Introduction

Mining terminological information from free or semi-structured text in large-scale technical corpora is slowly becoming a reasonably mature NLP technology, with term extraction systems leading the way. Automatically obtaining information *about* terms from free text has been a field less explored, but recent experiences have shown that compiling the extensive resources that modern scientific and technical disciplines need to manage the explosive growth of their knowledge is both feasible and practical. A good example of this NLP-based processing need is the National Library of Medicine's MedLine abstract database, which incorporates around 40,000 new Life Sciences papers each month. In order to maintain and update UMLS knowledge resources[1] the NLM staff needs to manually review 400,000 highly-technical papers each year (Powell et al. 2002). Most of these terminological knowledge sources have been compiled from existing glossaries and vocabularies that might become dated fairly quickly, and elucidating this information from domain experts is not an option. Neology detection, terminological information update and other tasks can benefit from automatic search, in highly technical text, of semantic and pragmatic information, e.g. when new information about sublanguage usage is being put forward. In this paper we describe and evaluate the Metalinguistic Operation Processor (MOP) system, implemented to automatically create Metalinguistic Information Databases (or MIDs) from large collections of special-domain research and reference documents. Section 2 discusses previous work, while Section 3 provides an overview of metalinguistic exchanges between experts, and their role in the constitution of technical knowledge. Section 4 presents experiments to localize and disambiguate good candidate metalinguistic sentences, using rule-based and stochastic learning strategies. Section 5 focuses on the problem of identifying and structuring the different linguistic constituents and surface segments of metalinguistic predications. Finally, Section 6 offers a discussion of results and suggestions for possible applications and future lines of research.

2 Previous work

One of the constraints of recent lines of research (Pearson, 1998; Klavans et al., 2001; Pascual & Pery-Woodley, 1997) is their focus on definitions, a theoretical object that, although undoubtedly useful and extensively described, presents by its very nature certain limitations when studying expert-domain peer-to-peer communication.[2] The meaning normalization process inherent in

[1] The MeSH and SPECIALIST vocabularies, a Metathesaurus, a Semantic Network, etc.

[2] In some recent approaches, Meyer (2001) and Condamines & Rebeyrolles (2001) exploit wider lexico-conceptual relations in free-text that can be difficult to model and locate accurately.

compiling definitions may be desirable when creating human-readable reference sources, but might lead to a loss of valuable information for specific contexts where the term appears. Pragmatic information (valid usage conditions or contextual restriction for the terms), or purely evaluative statements (usefulness or validity of a certain term for its intended purpose), might not be found in *classical* definitional contexts. Metalinguistic information in texts can provide us with information not only about what terms mean, but also how they are actually used by domain experts. A wide spectrum of sentential realizations of these kinds of information has been reported by Meyer (2001) and Rodríguez (2001), and organizing it to provide useful terminological resources is left for manual review by human lexicographers. We believe that using the more general concept of metalanguage can automate as much as possible the extraction of fine-grained knowledge about terms, as well as better capture the dynamical nature of the evolution of the scientific and technical knowledge created through the interaction of expert-domain groups.

3 Metalanguage, terminology and scientific knowledge

3.1 Corpora used in our research

Preliminary empirical work to explore how researchers modify the terminological framework of their highly complex conceptual systems included an initial manual review of 19 sociology articles (138k words) in academic journals. We looked at how term introduction and modification was done, as well as how metalinguistic activity was signalled in text, both by lexical and paralinguistic means. Some of the indicators found included verbs and verbal phrases like *called, known as, defined as, termed, coined, dubbed*, and descriptors such as *term* and *word*. Non-lexical markers included quotation marks, apposition and text layout.[3] The metalinguistic patterns thus identified were expanded (using variations of lexemes, verbal tenses and forms) into 116 queries to the scientific and learned domains of the British National Corpus. The resulting 10,937 sentences (henceforth, the MOP corpus) were manually classified as metalinguistic or otherwise, with 5,407 (49.6% of total) found to be truly metalinguistic sentences, using the criteria described in Section 3.2 below.[4] Other corpora from different domains (described in Section 4) was used both in this preliminary analysis of metalinguistic exchanges, as well as in evaluation and development of the MOP system.

3.2 Explicit Metalinguistic Operations

Careful analysis of these corpora, as well of examples in other European languages, presented some interesting facts about what we have termed "Explicit Metalinguistic Operations" (or EMOs):[5]

A) EMOs do not usually follow the *genus-differentia* scheme of aristotelian definitions, nor conform to the rigid and artificial structure of lexicographic entries. More often than not, specific information about language use and term definition is provided by sentences such as (1), in which the term *trachea* is linked to the description *fine hollow tubes* in the context of a globally non-metalinguistic sentence:

(1) This means that they ingest oxygen from the air via fine hollow tubes, known as tracheae.

In research papers partial and heterogeneous information is much more common than complete definitions, although it might otherwise in textbooks geared towards learning a discipline.

B) Introduction of metalinguistic information in discourse is highly regular, regardless of the domain. This can be credited to the fact that the writer needs to mark these sentences for special processing by the reader, as they dissect across two different semiotic levels: a meta-language and its *object* language, to use the terminology of logic where these concepts originated.[6] Their

[3] Similar work by Pearson (1998) obtained many of the same patterns from the Nature corpus of exact science documents.

[4] Reliability of human subjects for this task has not been reported in the literature, and was not evaluated in our experiments.

[5] We have used the term to highlight the operational nature of such textual instances in technical discourse.

[6] Natural language has to be split (at least methodologically) into two distinct systems that share the same rules and elements: a metalanguage used to refer to an object language, which in turn can refer to and describe objects in the mind or in the physical world. The fact that the two are isomorphic accounts for reflexivity, the property of referring to itself, as when linguistic items are mentioned instead of being used normally in an utterance. Rey-Debove (1978)

constitutive ***markedness*** means that most of the times these sentences will have at least two indicators of metalinguistic nature. These formal and cognitive properties of EMOs facilitate the task of locating them accurately in text.

C) EMOs can be further analyzed into 3 distinct components, each with its own properties and linguistic realizations:

i) An **autonym** *(see note 6)*: One or more self-referential lexical items that are the logical or grammatical subject of a predication.

ii) An **informational segment**: a contribution of relevant information about the meaning, status, coding or interpretation of a linguistic unit. Informational segments constitute what we state about the autonymical element.

iii) **Markers/Operators:** Elements used to make prominent the whole discourse operation and its non-referential, metalinguistic nature. They are usually lexical, paralinguistic or pragmatic devices that articulate autonyms and informational segments into a predication.

In a sentence such as (2) we have marked the autonym with *italics*, the informational segment with **bold** type and the marker-operator items with square brackets:

(2) **The bit sequences representing quanta of knowledge** [will be called "] *Kenes* ["], **a neologism intentionally similar to 'genes'** .

3.3 Knowledge and knowledge of language

Whenever scientists advance the state of the art of a discipline, their language has to evolve and change, and this build-up is carried out under metalinguistic control. Previous knowledge is transformed into new scientific common ground and ontological commitments are introduced when semantic reference is established. That is why when we want to structure and acquire new knowledge we have to go through a resource-costly cognitive process that integrates within coherent conceptual structures and theories a considerable amount of new and very complex lexical items and terms. Technical terms are not, by definition, part of the far larger linguistic competence of a first native language. Unlike everyday words within a specific social group, terms are conventional, even if they have derived from a word that originally belonged to collective competence. We could even posit that all technical terms owe their existence to a baptismal speech act, and that given a big enough sample (an impossibly exhaustive corpus of all expert language exchanges), an initial metalinguistic sentence could be located that constitutes an original, foundational source of meaning.

The information provided by metalinguistic exchanges is not usually inferable from previous one available to the speaker's community, and does not depend on general language competence by itself, but nevertheless is judged important and relevant enough to warrant the additional processing effort involved. Computing what is relevant metalinguistic information has to be done dynamically by figuring out which terminological items can be assumed to be shared by all, and which are new or have to be modified. It's an extended and more complex instance of lexical alignment between interlocutors (Pickering & Garrod, in press). Observing closely how this alignment is achieved can allow us to create computer applications that mimic some aspects of our impressive human competence as efficient readers of technical subjects, as incredibly good lexical-data processors that constantly update and construct our own special purpose vocabularies.

4 Filtering out non-metalinguistic sentences: two NLP approaches

The first issue to tackle when mining metalanguage is how to obtain a reliable set of candidate sentences for input into the next extraction phases. We employ a "discourse-oriented" approach that differs from Meyer's (2001) "term-oriented" one. We do not assume we have initially identified a terminological unit and proceed from there, but rather we first locate a metalinguistic discourse operation where a term can be retrieved along with information that refers to it. Condamines & Rebeyrolles (2001) and Meyer (2001) both exploit patterns of "knowledge-rich contexts" to obtain semantic and conceptual information about terms, either to inform terminological definitions or provide structure for a terminological system. A key problem in such approaches that use lexical-based "triggers" is how to control the amount of "noise", or non-relevant instances. The experiments in this

---

follows Carnap in calling this condition *autonymy*.

section compare two different NLP techniques for this task: symbolic and statistic techniques.

From our initial analysis of various corpora we selected 44 patterns that showed the best statistical reliability as EMO indicators.[7] We started out by tokenizing text, which then was run through a cascade of finite-state devices that extracted a set of candidate sentences before filtering out non-metalinguistic instances. Our filtering distinguishes between useful results, e.g. using the lexical pattern *called* in (3) from non-metalinguistic instances in (4):

(3) Since the shame that was elicited by the coding procedure was seldom explicitly mentioned by the patient or the therapist, Lewis **called** it unacknowledged shame.

(4) It was Lewis (1971;1976) who **called** attention to emotional elements in what until then had been construed as a perceptual phenomenon .

We experimented with two strategies for disambiguation: first, we used collocations as added restrictions (e.g., verbal vs. nominal occurrences of our lexical markers) to discard non-metalinguistic instances, for example *attention* in sentence (4) next to the marker *called.* The next table shows a sample of the filtering collocations.

Preceding	Subsequent
for **calls**	
in, duty, personal, conference, local, next, the, their, house, anonymous, phone, telephone...	out, someone, charges, before, charge, back, contact, for, upon, to, into, off, 911, by...
for **coin**	
pound, small, pence, in, toss, the, this, a, that, one, gold, silver, metal, esophageal ...	toss

We also implemented learning algorithms trained on a subset from our EMO corpus, using as vectors either Part-of Speech tags or word strings, at one, two, and three positions adjacent before and after our lexical markers. Our evaluations are based on 3 document sets: a) our original exploratory sociology corpus [5,581 sentences, 243 EMOs]; b) an online histology textbook [5,146 sentences, 69 EMOs]; and c) a small sample from the MedLine abstract database [1,403 sentences, 10 EMOs]. Our system is coded in Python, using the NLTK platform (nltk.sf.net) and a Brill tagger by Hugo Liu at MIT.

4.1 The collocation-based approach

Our first approach fared well, with good precision numbers but not so encouraging recall. The sociology corpus gave 0.94 Precision (P) and 0.68 Recall (R), while the histology one presented 0.9 P and 0.5 R. These low recall numbers reflect the fact that we used a non-exhaustive list of metalinguistic patterns. Example (5) shows one kind of metalinguistic sentence attested in corpora that the system does not extract or process:

(5) “Intercursive” power, on the other hand, is power in Weber's sense of constraint by an actor or group of actors over others.

We also tested extraction against a golden standard where sentences that had patterns that our list was not designed to retrieve were removed, which gave a more realistic picture of how the extraction system worked for the actual dataset it was designed to consider. For the sociology corpus (and a ß factor of 1), P was 0.97 and R 0.79, with an F-measure of 0.87. In the histology one P was measured at 0.94, R at 0.81 and F-measure at 0.87. In order to better compare the two filtering strategies, we decided also to zoom in on a more limited subset of verb forms (namely, *calls, called, call*), which presented ratios of metalinguistic relevance in our MOP corpus ranging from 100% positives (for the pattern *so called* + quotation marks) to 31% (*call*). Restricted to these verbs, our metrics showed precision and recall rates around 0.97. One problem with this approach is that the hand-coded rules are domain-specific, and customization for other domains is labour-intensive. In our tests, although most of the collocations work language-wide (phrasal verbs or prepositions), some of them are very specific.[8] Although collocation-based filtering will result in a working system, customization is error-prone and laborious.

4.2 Testing learning algorithms

We selected the co-text of marker/operators as relevant features for classifiers based on well-known naive Bayes and Maximum Entropy algorithms that have been reported to work well

[7] We excluded dispositional and typographical clues from our selectional patterns, involving mainly lexica and punctuation.

[8] “esophageal coins” is quite unusual outside of medical documents.

with sparse data.[9] We used either as grammatical context the POS tags or the word forms immediately adjacent in one to three positions before and after our triggering markers. Testing all possible combinations evaluates empirically the ideal mix of algorithm, feature type and coverage that insures best accuracy. The naive Bayes algorithm estimates the conditional probability of a set of features given a label, using the product of the probabilities of the individual features given that label. It assumes that the feature distributions are independent, but it has been shown to work well in cases with high degree of feature dependencies. The Maximum Entropy model establishes a probability distribution favouring entropy or uniformity subject to the constraints encoded in the feature-known label correlation. To train our classifiers, Generalized and Improved Iterative Scaling algorithms were used to estimate the optimal maximum entropy of a feature set, given a corpus.[10] 1,371 training sentences from our MOP dataset were converted into YES-NO labelled vectors. The following example from the textual segment "*... creates what Croft calls a description constraint ...*", uses 3 positions and POS tags:

('VB WP NNP', 'calls', 'DT NN NN')/'YES'@[102].

The different number of positions to the left and right of our training sentences, as well as the nature of the features selected (there are many more word-types than POS tags) ensured that our 3-part vector introduced a wide range of features against our 2 possible labels. The best results of each algorithms restricted to the lexeme *call*, are presented in the next table. Figures 1 and 2 present best results in the learning experiments for the complete set of patterns used in the collocation approach, over two of our evaluation corpora.[11]

Type	Positions	Tags/Words	Features	Accuracy	Precision	Recall
GIS	1	W	1254	0.97	0.96	0.98
IIS	1	T	136	0.95	0.96	0.94
NB	1	T	136	0.88	0.97	0.84

[9] *see* Rish, 2001, Ratnaparkhi, 1997 and Berger et al, 1996 for a formal description of these algorithms.

[10] In other words, given known data statistics, construct a model that best represents them but is otherwise as uniform as possible.

[11] Legend: P: Precision; R: Recall; F: F-Measure. NB: naïve Bayes; IIS: Maximum Entropy with Improved Iterative Scaling; GIS: Maximum Entropy with Generalized Iterative Scaling. (Positions/Feature type)

Figure 1. Best metrics for Sociology corpus

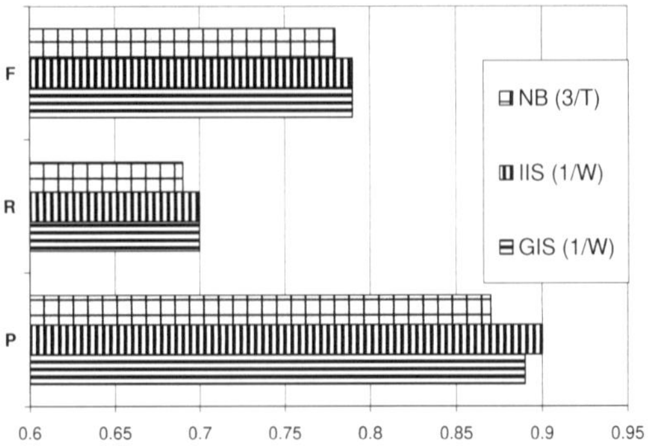

Figure 2. Best metrics for Histology corpus

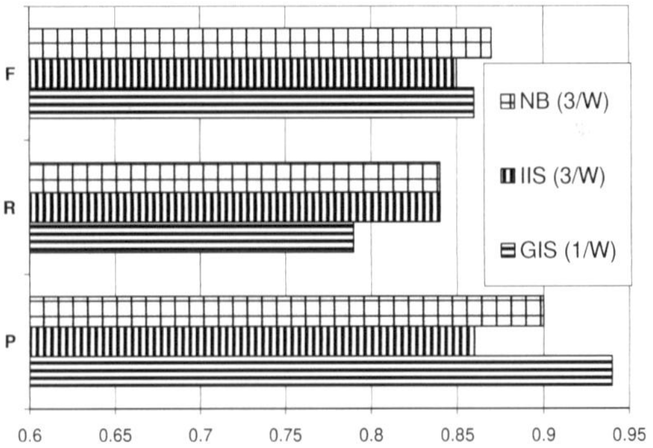

Although our tests using collocations showed that structural regularities would perform well, our intuitions about improvement using more features (more positions to the right or left of the lexical markers) or a more grammatically restricted environment (surrounding POS tags), turned out to be overly optimistic. Nevertheless, stochastic approaches that used short-range features did perform in line with the hand-coded approach. Both Knowledge-Engineering and supervised learning approaches were adequate for initial filtering of metalinguistic sentences, although learning algorithms might allow easier transport of systems into new domains.

5 From EMOs to metalinguistic databases

After EMOs were obtained, POS tagging, shallow parsing and limited PP-attachment are performed. Resulting chunks were tagged as *Autonyms, Agents, Markers, Anaphoric elements* or *Noun Chunks*, using heuristics based on syntactic, pragmatic and argument structure of lexica in the extraction patterns, as well as on FrameNet data in *Name conferral* and *Name*

Figure 4. Metrics for 3 corpora
(# of Records/Global F-Measure)

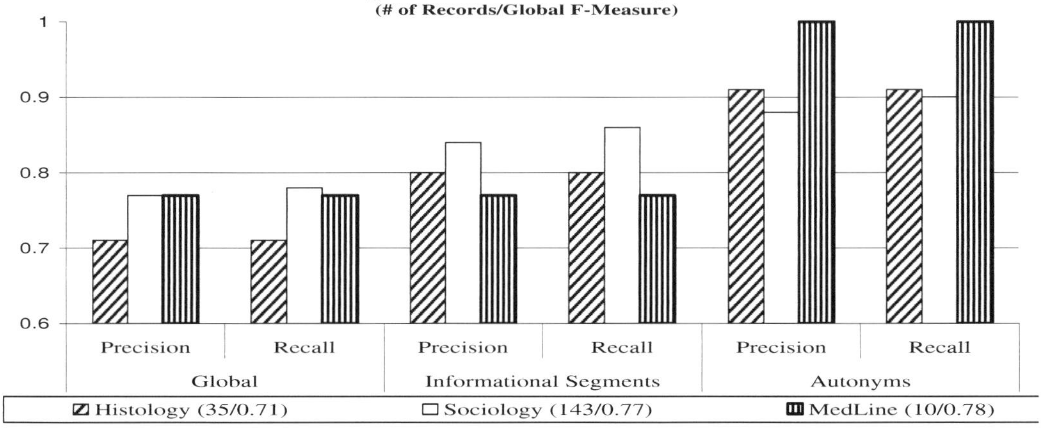

bearing frames. Next, a predicate processing phase selected the most likely surface realization for informational segments, autonyms and makers-operators, and proceeded to fill out the templates of the database. As mentioned earlier, informational segments present many realizations far from the completeness and conciseness of lexicographic entries. In fact, they may show up as full-fledged clauses (6), as inter- or intra-sentential anaphoric elements (7 and 8), as sortal information (9), or as an unexpressed "existential variable" (logical form ∃x) indicating only that certain discourse entity is being introduced (10):

(6) In 1965 the term soliton was coined **to describe waves with this remarkable behaviour**.

(7) This leap brings cultural citizenship in line with **what** has been called the politics of citizenship .

(8) **They** are called "endothermic compounds."

(9) One of the most enduring aspects of all social theories are **those conceptual entities** known as structures or groups.

(10) A [**∃x**] so called cell-type-specific TF can be used by closely related cells....

We have not included an anaphora-resolution module in our system, so that examples 7, 8 and 10 only output either unresolved surface elements or variable placeholders.[12] Nevertheless, more common occurrences like example sentence (1) are enough to create MIDs that constitute useful resources for lexicographers. The correct database entry for (1) is presented below.

Reference	Histology sample # 6
Autonym	*tracheae*
Information	*fine hollow tubes*
Markers/Operators	*known as*

To better reflect overall performance, we introduced a threshold of similarity of 65% for comparison between a golden standard slot entry and the one obtained by the application.[13] The final processing stage presented metrics shown in Figure 4. Our best numbers for informational segments ranged around 0.85, while the lowest were obtained for the histology corpus, with global precision and recall rates around 0.71, but with high numbers in the autonym identification task (0.91) and midrange ones for the informational segments (0.8). We observed that even though it is assumed that Bio-Medical Sciences have more consolidated vocabularies than Social Sciences, results for the MedLine and histology corpus occupy the extremes in the spectrum, with the sociology one in the middle range. The total number of candidate sentences was not a good predictor of system performance.

The DEFINDER system (Klavans et al., 2001) is to my knowledge the only one fully comparable with MOP, both in scope and goals, but with some significant differences.[14] Taking into account

---

[12] For sentence (8) the system might retrieve useful information from a previous one: "*A few have* ***positive enthalpies of formation.***"

[13] Thus, if the autonym or the informational segment is at least 2/3 of the correct response, it is counted as a positive, allowing for expected errors in the PP or acronym attachment algorithms.

[14] DEFINDER examines user-oriented documents

those differences, MOP compares well with the 0.8 precision and 0.75 recall of DEFINDER. While the resulting MOP "definitions" generally do not present high readability or completeness, these informational segments are not meant to be read by laymen, but used by domain lexicographers updating existing glossaries for neological change, or, in machine-readable form, by other applications.

6 Discussion and future work

We have chosen to exploit metalinguistic information that is being put forward in text because it can't be assumed to be part of the collective expert-domain competence. In doing so, we have exposed our system to the less predictable lexical environment of leading-edge research literature, the cauldron where knowledge and terminological systems are forged in real time, and where scientific meaning and interpretation are constantly debated, modified and agreed upon. We believe that low recall rates in our tests are in part due to the fact that we are dealing with the wider realm of metalinguistic information, as opposed to structured definitional sentences that have been distilled by an expert for consumer-oriented documents. We have not performed major customization of the system (like enriching the tagging lexicon with medical terms), in order to preserve the ability to use the system across different domains. Domain customization may improve metrics, but at a real cost for portability.

Conventional resources like lexicons and dictionaries compile meaning definitions that are considered stable and widely-shared. They can be seen as repositories of the default, core lexical information for terms used by a research community (that is, the information available to an average, idealized speaker). An MID, on the other hand, might contain the multi-textured real-time data embedded in research papers, and in this sense could be conceptualized as an *anti-dictionary*: a listing of exceptions, special contexts and specific usage of instances where meaning, value or pragmatic conditions have been spotlighted by discourse for cognitive reasons. Applications that rely on lookup on previously compiled resources would miss some of the data from EMOs, where the term is put forward for the first time, or where important, context-sensitive information about the terms is provided. MIDs cannot be viewed as end-user products, but as semi-structured resources (midway between raw corpora and structured lexical bases) that have to be further processed to convert them into usable data sources. We might better characterize them as auxiliary lexical knowledge resources, more than core lexical references. Lexicographers and terminologist can use them as tools for their own labour-intensive work of reviewing and compiling special-domain vocabularies.

MIDs could, in principle, also supply new interpretation rules in AI applications when inferences won't succeed because the state of the lexico-conceptual system has changed.[15] A neologism or a word in an unexpected technical sense could stump a NLP system that assumes it will be able to use the default information from a machine-readable dictionary or TKB. The kind of sortal information implicit in many definitions can also help improve anaphora resolution, semantic typing, acronym identification or bootstrapping of ontologies and taxonomies (Hearst, 1992; Condamines & Rebeyrolle, 2001; Pustejovsky et al., 2002; Malaisé et al. 2004). Although our approach might miss some of the important conceptual relations between terms, many of the MIDs we have obtained using language-centred contexts are rich sources of information. In addition, terminological information can be more specific than that obtainable by glossary lookup, and might be better suited for the interpretation of certain texts. The locality of such information can be seen as advantageous for specialized lexicography. Another area where non-standard information could prove useful is the study of the evolution of scientific sublanguages and the knowledge embodied by them. Changes in the

with fully-developed definitions for the layman. MOP focuses on leading-edge research papers that present less predictable templates. DEFINDER's qualitative evaluation criteria includes readability, usefulness and completeness, as judged by lay subjects, criteria which we have not adopted here, nor have we determined coverage against existing on-line dictionaries.

[15] When interpreting text, regular lexical information is applied by default under normal conditions, but more specific pragmatic or discursive information can override it if necessary, or if context demands so (Lascarides & Copestake, 1995).

conceptual and terminological configuration of a discipline might be traced and be better understood by the dynamical updates reflected in these databases. The next table shows a small sample, taken from our corpora, of that information's potential range, for some key concepts in the sociology domain.

Terms	Informational segments from EMOs
Family	extend the meaning to include same-sex couples, single-parents, nannies, adoptive and step children, and so on
Family	two adults of opposite sex, married to each other, and living with their common children
Identity	There are two typical contexts
Identity	an emotional attachment and a sense of belonging of a semi-sacred kind
Nationalism	used here, deliberately, to describe both aspects of the phenomenon
Nationalism	is used for both of these things - world view and activism

6.1 Conclusions

The implementation we have described here undoubtedly shows room for improvement: adding more patterns for better overall recall rates, deeper parsing for more accurate semantic typing of sentence arguments, etc. Also, the question of which learning algorithms can better perform the initial filtering of EMO candidates is still very much an open issue. We believe that the real challenge facing work such as this one lies not in retrieving EMOs from text to populate a MID, but in the successful formalization of heterogeneous linguistic information into a robust and manageable data structure. An effective and efficient computational representation of such diverse information is not trivial.

Nevertheless, we believe that applications focused on metalanguage, like the MOP system described here, can be very helpful for Terminology and lexicography, and that a MID's role would not be to replace, but to enrich and complement, Terminological Knowledge Bases.

References

Berger, A., S. Della Pietra et al. 1996. A Maximum Entropy Approach to Natural Language Processing. *Computational Linguistics*, v. 22, 1.

Condamines, A. & Rebeyrolle, J. 2001. Searching for and identifying conceptual relationships via a corpus-based approach to a Terminological Knowledge Base (CTKB). *Recent Advances in Computational Terminology*. John Benjamins.

Hearst, M. 1992. Automatic Acquisition of Hyponyms from Large Text Corpora. Proc. 14th Int. Conference on Computational Linguistics, Nantes, France.

Klavans, J. and Muresan, S. 2001. Evaluation of the DEFINDER System for Fully Automatic Glossary Construction, Proc. Am. Med. Inf. Ass. Symp.

Lascarides, A. and Copestake A. 1995. The Pragmatics of Word Meaning, in *Representation and Acquisition of Lexical Knowledge: Polysemy, Ambiguity and Generativity*. Stanford.

Malaisé V., Zweigenbaum P. & Bachimont, B. 2004. Repérage et exploitation d'énoncés définitoires en corpus pour l'aide à la construction d'ontologie. TALN 2004, Fès.

Meyer, I. 2001. Extracting knowledge-rich contexts for terminography. *Recent Advances in Computational Terminology*.

Pascual, E. & Péry-Woodley, M-P 1997. Modèles de texte pour la définition. Actes de Journées Scientifiques et Techniques du Réseau Francophone de l'Ingénierie de la Langue,

Pearson, J. 1998. Terms in Context. John Benjamins

Pickering, M. and Garrod, S. (in press) Toward a mechanistic psychology of dialogue. *Behavioral and Brain Sciences*. Cambridge University Press.

Powell, T., Srinivasan, S., et al. (2002) Tracking Meaning Over Time in the UMLS Metathesaurus. In *Biomedical Informatics: One Discipline*. Proc. Am. Med. Inf. Ass. Symp.

Pustejovsky J., A. Rumshisky and J. Castaño. 2002. Rerendering Semantic Ontologies: Automatic Extensions to UMLS through Corpus Analytics. LREC 2002, Spain.

Ratnaparkhi A., 1997. A Simple Introduction to Maximum Entropy Models for Natural Language Processing, TR 97-08, IRCS, University of Pennsylvania

Rish, I., 2001. An empirical study of the naive Bayes classifier, in IJCAI-01.

Rey-Debove, J. 1978. Le Métalangage. Le Robert, Paris.

Rodríguez, C. 2001. Parsing Metalinguistic Knowledge from Texts. *Selected papers from CICLING-2000* (IPN), Mexico.

Extracting Low-frequency Translation Pairs from Japanese-English Bilingual Corpora

Keita TSUJI
National Institute of Informatics
2-1-2 Hitotsubashi, Chiyoda-ku,
Tokyo 101-8430,
JAPAN
+81-3-4212-2571
keita@nii.ac.jp

Kyo KAGEURA
National Institute of Informatics
2-1-2 Hitotsubashi, Chiyoda-ku,
Tokyo 101-8430,
JAPAN
+81-3-4212-2518
kyo@nii.ac.jp

Abstract

We propose a method for extracting low-frequency translation pairs from Japanese-English bilingual corpora. Many methods have been proposed for extracting translation pairs from bilingual corpora, but most are based on word frequency and are, therefore, not effective in extracting low-frequency pairs. In Japanese-English corpora, many low-frequency translation pairs are loan-word pairs that can be extracted based on transliteration patterns. Our combined method, which relies on both transliteration and word frequency, performed significantly better than methods utilizing word frequency alone. Our method achieved 80% precision at 84% recall against the given corpus, while the word-frequency model achieved just 80% precision at 8% recall.

1 Introduction

In NLP application areas such as machine translation and cross-language information retrieval, a range of translation word pairs are needed. While popular and well-known translation pairs are included in existing bilingual dictionaries, newly coined and minor translation pairs are not yet covered in any resource. Therefore, it would be very useful if we could extract these pairs from proper bilingual corpora. Because newly coined translation pairs have just begun to appear in text and because of the nature of minor translation pairs, the frequencies of both are necessarily low. From this point of view, we aim to develop a method for extracting low-frequency translation pairs from Japanese-English bilingual corpora.

So far, there have been many methods proposed for extracting translation pairs from bilingual corpora. The most typical and intensively studied are word-frequency-based methods that extract word W_J and $W_{E\circ}$ as translation if W_J and $W_{E\circ}$ co-occur in numerous bilingual sentence pairs. Although frequency-based methods have a strong theoretical basis and are often sufficiently effective, they have one weak point, i.e., they are not good at extracting low-frequency pairs. For instance, if W_J and $W_{E\circ}$ occur and co-occur in just one bilingual sentence pair, and another word, $W_{E\times}$, occurs in one and the same sentence, the frequency-based method cannot determine which – $W_{E\circ}$ or $W_{E\times}$ – is the correct translation of W_J.

It is therefore desirable to develop a method for extracting low-frequency translation pairs, filling the gaps in, as well as making good use of, the frequency-based method. Language-pair-independent methods such as the frequency-based method are adequately refined, and we believe that incorporating language-pair-dependent knowledge, which is often ignored, is a step in the right direction. In this, among the first studies based on this framework, we focus on the Japanese and English language pair, although we take special care to keep the method as open to generalization as possible.

In Japanese-English bilingual corpora, many low-frequency translation pairs are loan-word pairs. Although these pairs can be extracted based on some transliteration patterns (without relying on word frequency) and there has been some research related to transliterations (Knight and Graehl, 1997)(Fujii and Ishikawa, 2001), few studies have been conducted for extracting these pairs from bilingual corpora based on transliteration. Two tasks arise: (1) To develop an effective method for extracting transliterated word pairs that include many of the low-frequency Japanese-English translation pairs; and (2) To make good use of the frequency-based method to extract low-frequency and especially non-transliterational translation pairs. Solving these tasks, we propose a combined method that utilizes both transliteration and word frequency.

In the following sections, we will first give the results of an investigation into low-frequency translation pairs, next describe our method, and then show that significant improvement was observed by our proposed method.

2 Preliminary Investigation

We used one bilingual dictionary and four bilingual corpora for our investigation and experiment. The bilingual dictionary we used was EDICT, which contained 102,380 pairs of Japanese-English translation pairs. We regard EDICT as one example of existing bilingual dictionaries.

The bilingual corpora we used consist of 9,000 pairs of abstracts of academic papers in the fields of (1) information processing field and (2) architecture collected by the National Institute of Informatics of Japan. Each Japanese-English abstract was written by the respective authors of each paper, and there is no strict correspondence between them. We assume that corpora which are strictly correspondent at each sentence level are still hard to obtain, while loosely correspondent ones become more readily available. [1] We chose these abstract corpora to keep our method realistic and applicable to many fields. Also, consequently, we do not try to align sentences in each abstract. Instead, we defined each whole abstract as a segment from which we extracted translation pairs. We also used 9,000 bilingual titles in the above fields for comparison. The basic quantities are shown in Table 1. [2] 'Inf-Abst' and 'Arc-Abst' represent the abstract corpus of information processing and architecture, respectively. 'Inf-Titl' and 'Arc-Titl' represent the title corpus in the same manner.

We define '$min(W_J, W_E)$' of the word pair W_J and W_E as the smaller of the number of segments in which the word W_J occurred and in which W_E occurred. For instance, if W_J and W_E occurred in four and six segments, respectively, '$min(W_J, W_E)$' of that pair is four. In addition, we represent the translation pairs whose $min(W_J, W_E)$ is N as '$min(W_J, W_E) = N$ *translation pairs*'.

We randomly selected 1,000 segments of each corpus and manually identified the translation pairs which should be extracted in each segment. In our estraction experiment, we evaluated the result based on these pairs. The number of these pairs are shown in the column 'Pair' in Table 5. For instance, we can see in Table 5 that there are 548 $min(W_J, W_E) = 1$ *translation pairs* in the information processing abstract corpus. Note that their frequencies were counted based on 9,000 segments, not on 1,000 segments.

[1] For instance, (Omae et al, 2003) obtained loosely correspondent bilingual texts from the Web by submitting bilingual equivalent keywords to Google and extracting translation pairs from the resultant texts.

[2] The plural forms of English words were converted into singular forms. ChaSen 2.0b and Brill tagger were used for the Japanese and English texts, respectively.

	Chasen Words		English Words	
	Token	Type	Token	Type
Inf-Abst	1,389,473	23,072	957,467	34,908
Arc-Abst	1,263,833	23,758	695,542	40,244
Inf-Titl	101,421	7,312	83,357	12,843
Arc-Titl	181,744	9,125	156,479	18,625

Table 1: Basic Quantities of Four Corpora

2.1 Existing Dictionary and Low-frequency Pairs in the Corpora

We investigated what percentages of the single word noun translation pairs in the corpora are listed in EDICT. The results are shown in the column 'R_Dict' in Table 5. Generally speaking, the low-frequency translation pairs (i.e., those whose $min(W_J, W_E)$ are small) are not listed in EDICT. For instance, only 11.78% of $min(W_J, W_E) = 1$ *translation pairs* in the architecture abstract corpus are listed in EDICT. With this fact, we would like to say that the existing bilingual dictionaries do not contain low-frequency translation pairs.

2.2 Problems With the Frequency-based Method for Extracting Low-frequency Pairs

We define 'full co-occurrence' of a word A with a translation pair (X, Y) as a situation in which the word A and X always co-occur in the same segment. There are two types of full co-occurrence: (a) A and X belong to the same language; and (b) A and X belong to different languages.

When type-(a) full co-occurrence as in Table 2 occurs (i.e., A='ノード', (X, Y)=('経路','path')), the frequency-based method estimates that '経路' and 'ノード' are equally likely to be the translation of 'path'. When type-(b) full co-occurrence as in Table 3 occurs (i.e., A='node', (X, Y)=('経路','path')), the frequency-based method estimates that 'node' is more likely to be the translation of '経路' than 'path'. In situations of type-(a), the method cannot determine which is the correct translation, and in situations of type-(b), the method chooses the wrong word as the translation.

Full co-occurrence is related to 'indirect association' (Melamed, 2000). But this only refers to situations in which word A 'often' – as opposed to 'fully' – co-occurs with X.

Table 5 shows how full co-occurrence can pose a difficult obstacle for the frequency-based method when extracting low-frequency translation pairs. In Table 5, 'R_Full_Cooc' is the ratio (%) of translation pairs that are fully co-occurred by other words against the total translation pairs. For instance, among 314 $min(W_J, W_E) = 1$ *translation pairs* in the architecture abstract corpus, 90.13% are fully co-occurred by other words.

Japanese Part	English Part
	path
経路, ノード	path
経路, ノード	path
経路, ノード	path
	path

Table 2: Full Co-occurrence of Type-(a)

Japanese Part	English Part
	path
経路	path, node
経路	path, node
経路	path, node
	path

Table 3: Full Co-occurrence of Type-(b)

2.3 Loan-word Pairs Among Low-frequency Pairs

The character types of translation pairs are also shown in Table 5. 'Katak', 'Roman', 'Kanji' and 'Other' represents the ratio (%) of the translation pairs whose Japanese words are represented using katakana characters, Roman alphabets, kanji characters and other characters, respectively. In the Japanese language, most of the transliterated loan words are written in katakana or the Roman alphabet, and vice versa. Table 5 shows that the smaller the $min(W_J, W_E)$ becomes, the larger the ratio of the loan-word pairs becomes. The loan-word pairs can be extracted based on some transliteration patterns without relying on word frequency.

3 The Extraction Method

Our preliminary investigations revealed: (1) that most of the low-frequency translation pairs are in the situation of full co-occurrence (as mentioned in Section 2.2) and cannot be extracted based on word frequency alone; and (2) that many of them are transliterated word pairs. Our method is based on these observations; it is as follows:

1) From each segment, extract the translation pairs based on transliteration. For instance, if there are candidate words '経路 (path)' and 'ノード (node)' in the Japanese part of the segment and there are 'path' and 'node' in the English part of the segment, 'ノード' and 'node' are extracted based on transliteration patterns such as 'ノ'='no' and 'ド'='de'.
2) Remove the extracted pairs from the candidate words. As a result, '経路' and 'path' are left in the segment.
3) Based on word frequency, extract translation pairs from the candidate words left in the segment.

Figure 1 shows the flow of our method.

Extraction methods like Steps 1 and 3 used to be studied independently. For instance, (Gale and Church, 1991)(Kupiec, 1993)(Smadja et al., 1996)(Hiemstra, 1997)(Kitamura and Matsumoto, 1996)(Ahrenberg et al., 1998)(Melamed, 2000) focused on word frequency and (Collier et al., 1997)(Jeong et al., 1999) extracted loan-word pairs based on transliteration patterns.

The unique point of our method in a technical sense is that we incorporated Steps 1 and 2 before applying the frequency-based method. These steps are the key to resolving the issue of full co-occurrence. We expect that Step 1 identifies the correct translation of A in Section 2.2 and Step 2 removes A with that correct translation. After these steps, the full co-occurrence by A is resolved and the frequency-based method regains its power to extract translation pairs (X, Y) that remain in the segment.

While many effective frequency-based methods have been proposed, there were only a few transliteration-based methods especially for the Japanese-English language pair. Against this background, the first author of the present paper developed an effective transliteration-based method (Tsuji, 2002). We adopted it for Step 1. As for Step 3, we adopted the method of (Melamed, 2000) and that of (Hiemstra, 1997). These were chosen because they seem to be the most sophisticated frequency-based methods at present. Note that they are just examples and other similar methods can be adopted as modules in Steps 1 and 3.

One technical problem is that if we extract and remove too many pairs at Steps 1 and 2, we are to wrongly extract Japanese-English word pairs as translations and pass insufficient candidates to Step 3. We assume that there exists optimal threshold for Steps 1 and 2 which can be determined empirically through our experiment.

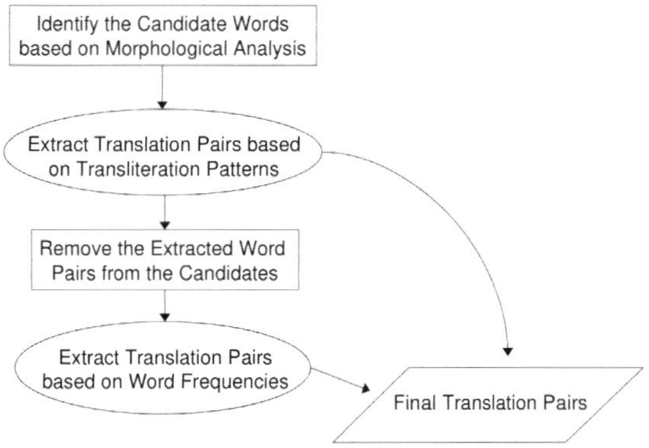

Figure 1: Flow of Extracting Translation Pairs

3.1 The Transliteration-based Method

Our method uses transliteration patterns that are observed in actual loan-word pairs (obtained from bilingual dictionaries, etc.). These patterns are obtained by breaking down the Japanese word into mora units (Japanese syllables) and manually identifying the corresponding character strings in the counterpart English word. Based on these patterns, we extract the loan-word pairs as follows:

(1) Decompose Japanese word W_J into mora units.

(2) Using all the existing transliteration patterns, generate all the back-transliteration candidates for W_J (henceforth, we represent the i-th candidate as $M_i(W_J)$).

(3) Pick up the English word W_E that co-occurred with W_J and identify the longest common subsequence with $M_i(W_J)$ ($\equiv C(M_i(W_J), W_E)$).

(4) If the following D exceeds a certain threshold, extract the pair W_J and W_E as translation (where $N(W)$ represents the number of characters of string W).

$$D = max_i \frac{N(C(M_i(W_J), W_E)) \times 2}{N(M_i(W_J)) + N(W_E)}$$

If we have transliteration patterns like in Table 4 and W_J is 'グラフ', $3 \times 5 \times 4$ back-transliteration candidates such as <graf>, <graph>, ..., <gulerfe> are obtained. And if W_E is 'graph':

$$\begin{aligned} D &= max(\frac{N(C(\text{graf}, \text{graph})) \times 2}{N(\text{graf}) + N(\text{graph})}, \\ &\qquad \frac{N(C(\text{graph}, \text{graph})) \times 2}{N(\text{graph}) + N(\text{graph})}, \\ &\qquad \ldots \\ &\qquad \frac{N(C(\text{gulerfe}, \text{graph})) \times 2}{N(\text{gulerfe}) + N(\text{graph})}) \\ &= max(0.67, 1.00, ..., 0.33) \\ &= 1.00 \end{aligned}$$

It indicates that 'グラフ' and 'graph' are very likely to be translation. This method is more effective than that of (Collier et al., 1997). The main reason is that the transliteration patterns are more realistic and we take into account the length of $M_i(W_J)$.

グ	g	gue	gu		
ラ	ra	ru	la	lu	ler
フ	f	ph	ff	fe	

Table 4: Transliteration Patterns

3.2 The Frequency-based Method

The method of (Melamed, 2000) and that of (Hiemstra, 1997) link the word W_J and W_E as translation based on iterative algorithms. We extracted a word pair as translation if its score P was high:

$$P = \log(L(W_J, W_E) + 1) \frac{L(W_J, W_E) \times 2}{L(W_J, .) + L(., W_E)}$$

where $L(W_J, W_E)$ is the number of links between W_J and W_E at the convergence stage.

$L(W_J, .)$ is the sum of the number of links between W_J and all the other words. $L(., W_E)$ is defined as the same.[3]

4 Extraction Experiment

Two kinds of extraction experiments were performed. The targets of extraction were $min(W_J, W_E) = 1$ *translation pairs*, which we think are difficult to extract but believe to be valuable pairs in the sense that they include the most newly coined translation pairs.

As we previously-mentioned, we evaluated the result based on the randomly-selected 1,000 segments in the corpus. From the extracted pairs, we eliminated the pairs that could not be extracted from these 1,000 segments and calculated the precision and recall. We calculated them every time we extracted one pair whose P was highest at Step 3.

(A) Basic Extraction Experiment: We extracted $min(W_J, W_E) = 1$ *translation pairs* and evaluated the result. The threshold D at Steps 1 and 2 were 0.9 or 0.8. This experiment was performed to show the overall effectiveness of our method to extract low-frequency translation pairs.

(B) Non-transliterational Pairs Extraction Experiment: We evaluated the result of extracting $min(W_J, W_E) = 1$ *translation pairs* that were not loan-word pairs. This experiment was performed to show the effectiveness of incorporating Steps 1 and 2 before Step 3. If our method extracted these non-transliterational pairs with higher precision and recall than the frequency-based method alone, it is very likely that part of the issue of full co-occurrence was resolved through Steps 1 and 2. The threshold D at Steps 1 and 2 were 0.9, 0.8 or 0.7.

4.1 Result of the Basic Experiment

The results of the basic experiment against the information processing abstract corpus and the architecture abstract corpus are shown in Figures 2 and 3, respectively. In Figures 2 and 3, 'TLS(D=X)+Melamed' represents the precision and recall curve of the method whose threshold at Step 2 was X and whose frequency-based method used at Step 3 was that of (Melamed, 2000). Just 'Melamed' represents the result of using the method of (Melamed, 2000) alone. The notation of Hiemstra is the same. From Figures 2 and 3, we can say the following:

(1) The results gained through the frequency-based methods alone are not good. One of the reasons for this should be the issue of full co-occurrence.

(2) The results of the combined method are by far better than those of the frequency-based method only. For instance, the combined method (TLS(D=0.8)+Melamed) achieved 80% precision at 84% recall against the information processing abstract corpus while the method of (Melamed, 2000) achieved 80% precision at just 8% recall. Incorporating the transliteration-based method to extract Japanese-English seems to have been effective, as we hypothesized in our preliminary investigation.

(3) Generally speaking, the recall against the information processing abstract corpus was better than that against the architecture corpus. Table 5 shows that the amount of loan-word pairs in the information processing corpus is larger than that in the architecture corpus. The extraction result indicates that our method will function more effectively in fields or language pairs where word loans are common.

(4) The maximum of the recall when we set $D = 0.8$ was larger than that when we set $D = 0.9$. It means that, to achieve overall good recall, we should rely on transliteration-based method and greedily extract loan-word pairs.

These tendencies were also observed in the results against two title corpora, though the precision and recall were higher.

4.2 Result of Extracting Non-transliterational Pairs

The results of the experiment (B) against the information processing abstract corpus and the architecture abstract corpus are shown in Figures 4 and 5, respectively. We can see in Figure 4 that the performance of the combined method for extracting non-transliterational pairs is better than that of (Melamed, 2000) alone. For instance, the combined method (TLS(D=0.8)+Melamed) achieved 64% precision at 2% recall, while the method of (Melamed, 2000) achieved 19% precision at 2% recall. Similar results were obtained in other corpora and when we used the method of (Hiemstra, 1997). This indicates that Steps 1 and 2 resolved a number of cases of full co-occurrence among non-transliterational $min(W_J, W_E) = 1$ *translation pairs* and enabled the frequency-

[3] We adopted the method 'B' of (Melamed, 2000). We tried his '$score_B$' as the final criteria, too, but the above score P produced better results.

based method to extract them.

We can see in Figures 5 that the precision when we set $D = 0.9$ was lower than those when we set $D = 0.8$ and $D = 0.7$. It means that if we extract and remove only the highly-matched loan-word pairs, the full co-occurrence is not resolved. We observed that the best value for D was around 0.8.

5 Conclusions

From the standpoint that the low-frequency translation pairs in bilingual corpora include many useful pairs, we developed a method for extracting them from corpora. The investigation and experiment clarified the following four points: (1) The frequency-based method is not effective in extracting low-frequency translation pairs because of full co-occurrence; (2) In Japanese-English bilingual corpora, low-frequency translation pairs are often loan-word pairs and they can be extracted using the transliteration-based method; (3) The performance of the combined method for extracting low-frequency translation pairs is higher than that of the frequency-based method alone; (4) Extracting and removing the loan-word pairs using the transliteration-based method leads to the resolution or amelioration of full co-occurrence and enables the frequency-based method to extract non-transliterational low-frequency pairs.

What is special about our research is that it focused on word pairs that have often been ignored and that it proposed a method addressing the circumstances of the Japanese-English language pair quite well. We feel more attention should be paid to language-pair-dependent knowledge and we developed an optimized method for Japanese and English based on this framework. We would like to add that, by modifying the transliteration patterns, similar methods should work fairly well against other language pairs where word loans are common.

References

L. Ahrenberg et al. 1998. "A Simple Hybrid Aligner for Generating Lexical Correspondences in Parallel Texts". In *Proceedings of the COLING-ACL'98*, pages 29–35.

J. Breen. EDICT. http://www.csse.monash.edu.au/~jwb/.

N. Collier et al. 1997. "Acquisition of English-Japanese Proper Nouns from Noisy-Parallel Newswire Articles Using KATAKANA Matching". In *Proceedings of the Natural Language Processing Pacific Rim Symposium 1997*, pages 309–314.

A. Fujii and T. Ishikawa. 2001. "Japanese/English Cross-Language Information Retrieval: Exploration of Query Translation and Transliteration". *Computers and the Humanities*, 35(4):389–420.

W. A. Gale and K. W. Church. 1991. "Identifying Word Correspondences in Parallel Texts". In *Proceedings of the DARPA Speech and Natural Language Workshop*, pages 152–157.

D. Hiemstra. 1997. "Deriving a Bilingual Lexicon for Cross-Language Information Retrieval". In *Proceedings of the Fourth Groningen International Information Technology Conference for Students*, pages 21–26.

K. S. Jeong et al. 1999. "Automatic Identification and Back-transliteration of Foreign Words for Information Retrieval". *Information Processing and Management*, 35(4):523–540.

M. Kitamura and Y. Matsumoto. 1996. "Automatic Extraction of Word Sequence Correspondences in Parallel Corpora". In *Proceedings of the 4th Workshop on Very Large Corpora*, pages 79–87.

K. Knight and J. Graehl. 1997. "Machine Transliteration". In *Proceedings of the 35th Annual Conference of the ACL*, pages 128–135.

J. Kupiec. 1993. "An Algorithm for Finding Noun Phrase Correspondences in Bilingual Corpora". In *Proceedings of the Sixth Conference of the EACL*, pages 17–22.

I. D. Melamed. 2000. "Models of Translational Equivalence among Words". *Computational Linguistics*, 26(2):221–249.

H. Omae et al. 2003. "Extraction of Compound Word Translations from Non-parallel Japanese-French Text in World Wide Web". In *Proceedings of the Workshop PAPILLON-2003 on Multilingual Lexical Databases.* (No Pagenation).

F. Smadja et al. 1996. "Translating Collocations for Bilingual Lexicons: A Statistical Approach". *Computational Linguistics*, 22(1):1–38.

K. Tsuji. 2002. "Automatic Extraction of Translational Japanese-KATAKANA and English Word Pairs from Bilingual Corpora". *International Journal of Computer Processing of Oriental Languages*, 15(3):261–279.

Corpus	$min(W_J, W_E)$	Pair	R_Dict	R_Full_Cooc	Katak	Roman	Kanji	Other
Inf-Abst	1	548	8.76	84.12	17.15	55.47	14.96	12.41
	2	236	22.03	17.80	23.31	50.00	19.92	6.78
	3	150	24.00	7.33	16.67	47.33	26.00	10.00
	4	151	29.14	2.65	17.22	47.68	28.48	6.62
	5–9	425	40.47	0.94	24.00	30.12	39.06	6.83
	10+	1,907	62.87	0.05	21.31	24.47	48.11	6.12
Arc-Abst	1	314	11.78	90.13	25.48	18.79	46.50	9.24
	2	147	25.85	19.05	28.57	16.33	49.66	5.44
	3	102	37.25	3.92	30.39	12.75	50.00	6.86
	4	51	49.02	0.00	31.37	7.84	56.86	3.92
	5–9	230	48.26	0.43	18.26	6.96	72.17	2.61
	10+	1,357	67.65	0.00	15.81	6.36	73.65	4.18
Inf-Titl	1	248	17.34	55.65	18.95	35.08	35.89	10.08
	2	102	27.45	18.63	19.61	39.22	34.31	6.86
	3	79	43.04	3.80	17.72	22.78	50.63	8.86
	4	63	49.21	0.00	34.92	12.70	47.62	4.76
	5–9	181	45.86	0.00	24.72	5.39	68.03	1.86
	10+	538	61.52	0.00	22.05	17.84	55.08	5.04
Arc-Titl	1	147	21.77	55.78	32.65	12.24	50.34	4.76
	2	81	30.86	17.28	22.22	13.58	60.49	3.70
	3	48	52.08	8.33	33.33	10.42	54.17	2.08
	4	44	65.91	2.27	20.45	4.55	72.73	2.27
	5–9	153	60.78	0.65	16.99	2.61	77.78	2.61
	10+	588	66.50	0.17	15.93	4.52	77.29	2.26

Table 5: Translation Pairs in Dictionary, Fully Co-occurred and Their Character Types

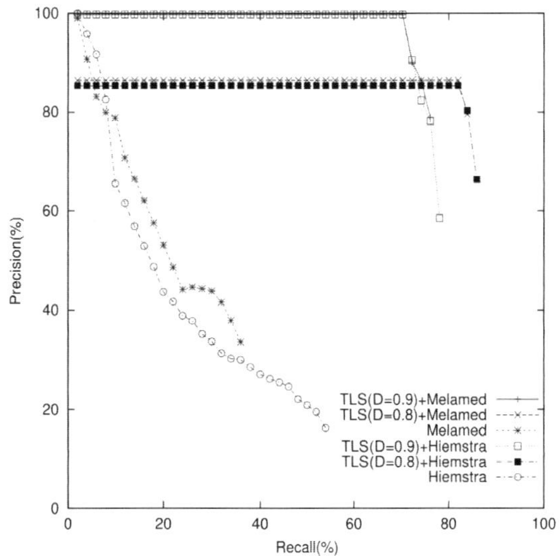

Figure 2: Extracting $min(W_J, W_E) = 1$ *Translation Pairs* (Inf-Abst)

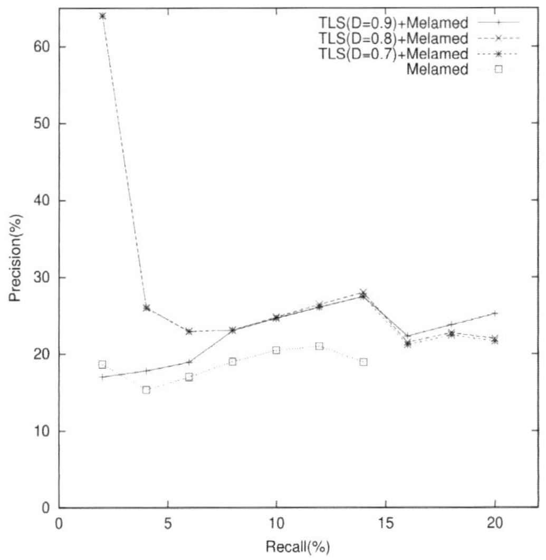

Figure 4: Extracting Non-transliterational $min(W_J, W_E) = 1$ *Translation Pairs* (Inf-Abst)

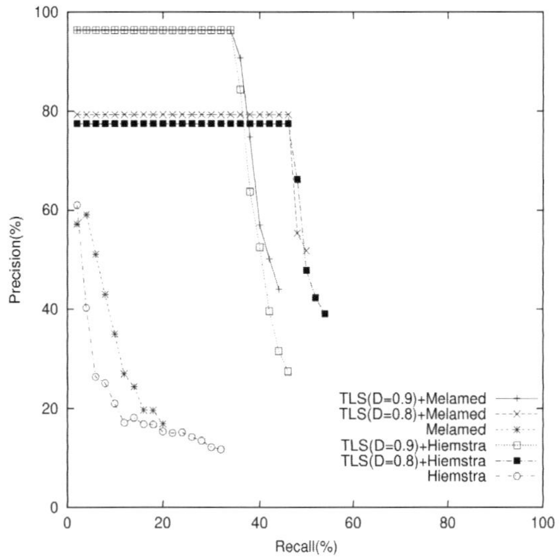

Figure 3: Extracting $min(W_J, W_E) = 1$ *Translation Pairs* (Arc-Abst)

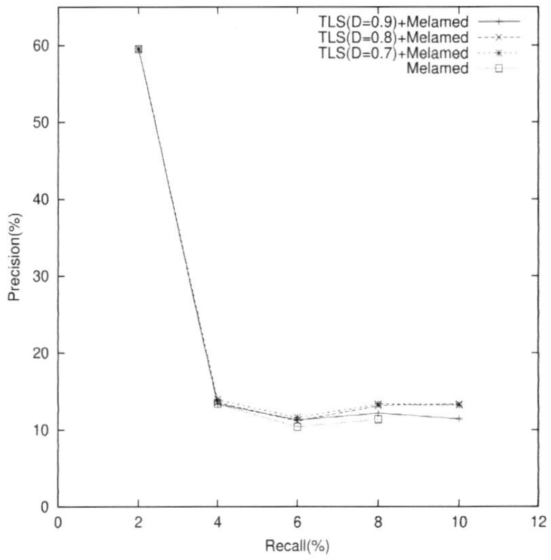

Figure 5: Extracting Non-transliterational $min(W_J, W_E) = 1$ *Translation Pairs* (Arc-Abst)

Dependence Relationships between Gene Ontology Terms based on TIGR Gene Product Annotations

Anand KUMAR
IFOMIS, Faculty of Medicine,
University of Leipzig,
Haertelstrasse 16-18
Leipzig, Germany, D-04107
anand.kumar@ifomis.uni-leipzig.de
URL:
http://www.uni-leipzig.de/~akumar/

Barry SMITH[1,2]
[1]IFOMIS, Faculty of Medicine,
University of Leipzig,
Haertelstrasse 16-18
Leipzig, Germany, D-04107
[2]Department of Philosophy,
SUNY at Buffalo,
Buffalo, NY 14260, USA
phismith@buffalo.edu
URL:
http://ontology.buffalo.edu/smith//

Christian BORGELT
Department of Knowledge
Processing and Language
Engineering, Otto-von-Guericke
University of Magdeburg,
Universitätsplatz 2,
Magdeburg, Germany, D-39106
christian.borgelt@cs.uni-magdeburg.de
URL:
http://fuzzy.cs.uni-magdeburg.de/~borgelt/

Abstract

The Gene Ontology is an important tool for the representation and processing of information about gene products and functions. It provides controlled vocabularies for the designations of cellular components, molecular functions, and biological processes used in the annotation of genes and gene products. These constitute three separate ontologies, of cellular components), molecular functions and biological processes, respectively. The question we address here is: how are the terms in these three separate ontologies related to each other? We use statistical methods and formal ontological principles as a first step towards finding answers to this question.

1 Introduction

(Zhu et al 2004) noted that creating a model of the dynamics of molecular interaction networks offers enormous potential for understanding systems biology. Existing work has led to the development of databases and ontologies which provide classifications and annotations based on a gene product's function, location, structure and so on, as for example in PANTHER (Thomas PD et al 2003), a library of protein families and subfamilies indexed by function, and the Gene Ontology Annotation[1] (GOA) (Camon et al 2003).

Further progress requires a robust formal ontology of structures, locations, functions and processes, linked together via relations such as *is_part_of*, *is_located_at*, *is_realized_by*, and so forth. As a step along this road, we provide a methodology for deriving and representing association rules between the entities present within the separate ontologies of the Gene Ontology.[2] (Gene Ontology Consortium, 2001). Such rules will be able to situate a biological process in relation to a cellular location to an agent. They will be able to relate lower-granularity molecular functions in relation to higher-granularity biological processes, and establish other sorts of relations between entities in different parts of GO.

A preliminary study in this area (Burgun et al 2004) combines ontological, lexical and statistical principles. Their study provides association rules on a selected set of 23 gene products that were potentially involved in enterocyte differentiation and that showed similar levels of expression. (Clelland and Oinn) provide commonly annotated terms based on the CluSTr database (Kriventseva et al 2001), which has recently been incorporated into the QuickGO browser.[3] Association rules have been used for mining gene expression data by (Creighton and Hanash 2003). (Ogren et al 2004) studied the compositional nature of the GO terms and described the dependencies among them.

Our investigation draws on the fact that terms from GO's separate ontologies are often used to annotation the same gene or gene product. We draw on the TIGR database to establish the corresponding patterns of association between terms in GO when taken in its entirety.

In what follows we describe the results of this work We analysed all of TIGR's 84,833

[1] http://www.ebi.ac.uk/GOA/

[2] http://www.geneontology.org/

[3] http://www.ebi.ac.uk/ego/

annotations, pertaining to the 41,502 distinct gene products present within GOA and focusing on the TIGR database within the February 2004 edition of GO. These associations were mined to establish association links between GO terms using standard statistical database techniques based on the so-called apriori algorithm and using a part of speech tagger. The discovered links were then analysed on the basis of methods drawn from foundational ontology.

2 Gene Ontology

2.1 The Cellular Component Ontology

GO's *cellular component* (cc) vocabulary consists of terms such as *flagellum*, *chromosome*, *ferritin*, *extracellular matrix* and *virion*. This ontology is the GO counterpart of anatomy within the medical framework. GO includes in this vocabulary both the extracellular environment of cells and the cells themselves (that is, *cell* is subsumed in GO by *cellular component*).

2.2 The Molecular Function Ontology

GO's definition of *molecular function* (mf) is: "the action characteristic of a gene product." The mf vocabulary accordingly subsumes terms describing actions, for example: *ice nucleation*, *binding*, or *protein stabilization*.

2.3 The Biological Process Ontology

A *biological process* (bp) is defined in GO as: "A phenomenon marked by changes that lead to a particular result, mediated by one or more gene products". Terms in bp can be quite specific (*glycolysis*) or very general (*death*). GO's mf and bp terms are clearly closely interrelated. The biological process of *anti-apoptosis*, for example, certainly involves the molecular function now labelled *apoptosis inhibitor activity*. Such molecular functions should stand to biological processes in a *part-of* relation. At the same time, however, GO's authors insist that *part-of* holds only between entities within a single vocabulary, and they thus provide no guidance as to the cross-vocabulary relations between the terms. We published a series of papers pointing out these and similar problems in GO as currently constituted (Smith et al 2004; Smith et al 2003; Kumar and Smith 2004; Kumar and Smith 2003).

3 TIGR database annotations

The Institute for Genome Research (TIGR)'s Genome Projects are a collection of curated databases containing DNA and protein sequence, gene expression, cellular role, protein family, and taxonomic data for microbes, plants and humans. (http://www.tigr.org/) TIGR has manually curated GO annotation for 6 bacterial genomes (V. cholerae, S. oneidensis, B. anthracis, G. sulfurreducens, P. syringae, and C. burnetii) and two eukaryotes (Arabidopsis thaliana, and Trypanosoma brucei). In addition, automated annotation has effected for Expressed Sequence Tags from several species.

The TIGR database is a rich source of information about gene indices based on genetic sequence. TGICL is a pipeline for the analysis of large Expressed Sequence Tags (EST) and mRNA databases in which the sequences are first clustered on the basis of pairwise sequence similarity and then assembled by individual clusters (Pertia et al 2003). Association rules between GO terms will enable us to determine the clusters of gene expression functions and locations in a way that will add to the knowledge that is contained within representations of such clusters on the basis of the gene indices only.

4 Methods

Associations between GO terms were established on the basis of the annotations in the TIGR databases.

4.1 Statistical approach

All the annotations from the TIGR database present within GO's association table were selected and placed into a separate table GO terms were then separated into three separate tables, depending on which of the three GO vocabularies they belong to.

Those GO terms which belong to two different ontologies within GO but are annotated to the same gene products were then separated out for analysis. Three new tables were then created containing those annotations where cc and mf terms, mf and bp terms, and cc and bp terms are annotated together.

The distinct term tuples present were grouped together and their count was used to provide a measure for weighting an association – which is to say how many times two GO terms from two distinct axes are annotated together (Table 1). The co-occurrence of terms within the annotations were then combined together (Table 2).

Cellular Component	Molecular Function	Weight
extrachromosomal circular DNA	DNA binding	3
provirus	transcription factor activity	6

Table 1. Associations between terms belonging to cc and mf, together with an index of how many times such associations occur within the annotation

Cellular Component	Biological Process	Molecular Function	Weight
nucleus	chromosome segregation	ATP binding	19
chloroplast stroma	signal transduction	MAP kinase activity	33

Table 2. Associations between terms belonging all three of GO's ontologies with an index of how many times such associations occur within the annotation

GO's hierarchy has thus far not been considered. Rather we have focused only on the terms themselves to which the annotations are made. For each GO term used for annotation and for each subsuming term in GO's *is_a* hierarchy, we can establish the distance of the former from the latter. (Resnik 1995) has pointed out that the semantic similarity of terms as one traverses the hierarchical tree reduces by a factor of log(p(c)) where p(c) is the probability of finding a child for the term when seeking information. Table 3 thus represents a quantification of this semantic similarity, which can be used to extend the results presented here by using an approach similar to that advanced in (Azuahe and Bodenreider, 2004).

Cellular Component	Molecular Function	Distance
DNA polymerase complex	Epsilon DNA polymerase activity	1
oxoglutarate dehydrogenase complex	oxoglutarate dehydrogenase (lipoamide) activity	1

Table 3. Associations between GO terms belonging to cc and mf taking hierarchy into consideration

4.2 Association rule induction

Association rule induction was originally developed for so-called market basket analysis, which aims at finding regularities in the shopping behaviour of customers of supermarkets, mail-order companies, online stores etc. (Borgelt and Kruse, 2002) Association rules are designed to help in isolating those sets of products that are frequently bought together. This information is expressed in the form of rules like "A customer who buys bread and wine is likely to buy cheese also."

Algorithms for inducing association rules from a set of transactions (the market baskets or shopping carts bought by customers) usually work in two steps: First, the so-called frequent item sets are determined by searching the subset lattice of all items. For this search there are, in principle, two approaches: the *breadth first* search, as employed by the apriori algorithm (Agrawal et al. 1994), and the *depth first* search, on which the eclat algorithm (Zaki et al. 1997) is based. Second, rules are constructed from the frequent item sets and filtered with respect to some quality criterion.

In the GO context, we use association rule induction to discover links between the ontologies in which a gene product is described. That is, we are interested in rules that predict cc from mf or bp, or rules that describe which mfs in which ccs constitute a bp, and so forth.

4.2.1 Assessment of association rules

The number of combinatorially possible rules here is very high. Consequently we need criteria to assess and thus to filter out those association rules which are of serious importance. The standard measures for this purpose are the *support* and the *confidence* of a rule.

The support of an association rule can be defined in two different ways: as the fraction of all transactions to which the rule is applicable (that is, which contain all items in the antecedent of the rule) or the fraction of all transactions for which the rule is correct (that is, which contain *all* items appearing in the rule, regardless of whether in antecedent or consequent). We take the second approach.

The confidence of an association rule is the fraction of cases in which it is correct relative to those in which it is applicable, that is, the ratio of the number of transactions that contain all items in the rule to the number of transactions that contain all items in the antecendent.

A user controls the search for association rules by providing minimum values for support and confidence of the rules to be found. From these values there can be derived a pruning criterion for the search for frequent item sets in the subset lattice as well as filtering criteria for the rules themselves. Only rules that meet both criteria are reported. More intuitively: we are looking for association rules that can be applied often (are above some minimum level of support) and that make reliable predictions (are above some minimum level of confidence).

4.2.2 Application to Gene Ontology

In our application of association rule induction to the analysis of GO we viewed each gene product annotated to a GO term as a transaction. We thus have as many transactions as there are gene products in the data set. We then looked for frequent co-occurrences of terms within such transactions and reported them in the form of association rules. For the search itself we used a well-known implementation of the apriori algorithm by (Borgelt and Kruse 2002).

In addition to filtering based on minimum support and minimum confidence, we also introduced one further selection criterion by requiring that the consequent of a rule must come from a different GO ontology than the terms in the antecedent of the rule, since rules containing only terms from one ontology are likely to recover only the term hierarchy of that ontology, which is not what is needed here. Such filtering can be achieved with the apriori implementation we used via the specification of which part of an association rule an item may appear in.

4.3 Experimental results

We ran the apriori program three times, each time restricting the consequent of the rules to a different ontology. This was required as GO has three orthogonal ontologies and one needed to treat each of them as an antecedent and a consequent with one another. Examples of rules we found are:

membrane [cc]
← oligopeptide transport [bp];
transporter activity [mf]
(0.106%/44, 100.0%)

binding [mf]
← mitochondrial transport [bp];
mitochondrial inner membrane [cc]
(0.106%/44, 100.0%)

protein biosynthesis [bp]
← ribosome [cc];
structural constituent of ribosome [mf]
(0.504%/209, 90.4%)

The two letters in brackets after each term denote the axis the term comes from. The numbers in parentheses at the end of each rule describe the quality of the rule as (S%/A, C%), where S is the support of the rule as a percentage of gene products to which the rule is applicable, A is the absolute number of gene products to which it is applicable (which is designed to complement the information regarding support), and C is the confidence of the rule.

In the GO context S is the percentage of gene product IDs to which the relevant rule is applicable (i.e., the percentage of gene product IDs which are annotated with all the terms in the antecedent in the rule), A is the absolute number of gene product IDs to which the rule is applicable, and C is the percentage of gene product IDs for which the rule makes the correct prediction relative to those to which the rule is applicable. Thus for example:

ribosome [cc]
← ribosome biogenesis [bp];
protein biosynthesis [mf]
(0.212%/88, 93.2%)

tells us that 88 gene product IDs (~0.2%) are annotated with the terms *ribosome biogenesis* and *protein biosynthesis*, of which 93.2% (i.e. 82) are also annotated with the term *ribosome*.

4.4 Dependencies based on Part-of-speech Tagging:

The terms within GO were tagged with a part-of-speech tagger Qtag[4] (Mason, 2004) in order to understand the linguistic dependencies between the terms (for example, between adjective and noun or between adverb and verb).

We tagged all the GO terms and also their definitions. The definition tags supplement the GO term tags since definitions are more elaborate and the specificity of the tagger also increases when it deals with complete sentences rather than with the collections of words by which GO terms are constituted.

Among the terms, we find 1813 adjectives, 29 adverbs, 2808 nouns, 11 prepositions and 57 verbs. Among the term definitions, we found 3460 adjectives, 252 adverbs, 4837 nouns, 21 prepositions and 595 verbs. The lowest specificity is found for chemical names.

Unfortunately very few of the interesting part-of-speech generated dependencies can be captured on the basis of an analysis of GO terms alone. This is because there are very few cases of such dependencies where both terms involved are present within GO. Examples are: *heme transport* and *heme transporter activity* or *growth* and *invasive growth.* In many other cases, however, we have complex GO terms whose constituents are not themselves present in GO. Thus *photoreactive repair* is present, but not *repair* or *photoreaction. Hypersensitive response* is present but not *response* and *hypersensitivity*. Terms like *during*, *within* and *without* play an important role in GO's compositional structure, but they are not themselves present within GO. (For more examples see (Smith et al. 2004).) To rectify this defect and to make the corresponding information accessible to software applications ways must be found to link GO to third-party ontologies in which the corresponding constituent terms are themselves subjected to formal treatment.

[4] http://web.bham.ac.uk/O.Mason/software/tagger/

Our statistical approach, apriori-generated association rules and lexical tagging yielded a range of different sorts of associations, for example between a location and a process, a process and a function, a function and another function, a process and another process, an agent and a function and so on. One needs a formal ontology, too, in order to express those relations within a single framework and thus to create a robust representation scheme that can serve as the basis for automated reasoning.

5 Basic Formal Ontology

To do full justice to the information content of GO and to the rules we isolated requires a formal ontological scheme which encompasses both continuants and endurants, and both processes and functions, and which further has the facility to deal with entities found on different levels of granularity (here on the molecular, cellular, and whole-organism levels). Basic Foundational Ontology (BFO) is a framework of this type, the essentials of which can be summarized as follows.

BFO consists of two complementary ontologies, called SNAP (a snapshot ontology of continuant entities existing at a time) and SPAN (a four-dimensional ontology of processes unfolding themselves through time. (Smith and Grenon, forthcoming)

The entities recognized by SNAP ontologies have continuous existence in time, preserve their identity through change and exist in toto at every moment at which they exist at all. They include: independent SNAP entities (substances and their aggregates, parts, and boundaries), and dependent SNAP entities such as qualities, roles, conditions, functions, dispositions, powers, etc.

SPAN entities, in contrast, have temporal parts which means that they unfold themselves in successive phases and can be segmented via segmentation of the temporal intervals which they occupy. SPAN entities include processes in the narrow sense, as well as the instantaneous temporal boundaries of processes, the temporal extents of processes, and so on.

5.1 Formal-Ontological Relations

Formal relations are those types of relations which can traverse the SNAP-SPAN divide; thus they are relations which glue SNAP and SPAN entities together.

A number of parameters can then be used in the construction of sub-ontologies within the wider BFO framework:

– the ontologies from which the relata derive, expressed as an ordered list, called the *signature* of the relation

– the *directionality* of the relation

The principal signatures in the binary case are as follows:

– <SNAP, SNAP>
– <SPAN, SPAN>
– <SNAP, SPAN>
– <SPAN, SNAP>

The first two signatures comprehend relations between ontologies with different domains or granularities. The latter comprehend the relations of realization and participation for example between a function and the process which is its functioning, or between an activity and its agent.

Below, we present various relations which can exist between entities in GO and which were found on the basis of our analysis of the TIGR database. Some of the relations require extending the association rules to include those entities which are absent within GO but included within its compositional structure along the lines described above.

5.1.1 Relations with Signature <SNAP, SNAP> and <SPAN, SPAN>

Transgranular Part-Whole Relations: The relations crossing ontologies of different levels of granularity are pre-eminently relations of part and whole. The <SNAP, SNAP> relations between independent SNAP entities are already present within GO. Example: *nuclear inclusion body* part-of *nucleus*.

Our association rules uncovered transgranular part-whole relations between dependent SNAP entities. For example: *transposase activity* ← DNA *transposition* (1.2%/505, 91.5%). Unlike BFO however GO does not clearly distinguish between functions and processes; hence the above example should be interpreted as involving both a transgranular relation between SNAP dependent entities:

transposase function
← DNA *transposition function*

and a transgranular relation between SPAN entities:

transposase activity
← DNA *transposition function*

This does justice to the fact that DNA transposition activity consists of various activities as its parts, of which is transposase activity.

5.1.2 Relations with Signature <SNAP Independent, SPAN>

Participation: The relation of participation, for example of a runner in a race, is a species of dependence. There are different kinds of participation, which we can order along the following dimensions:

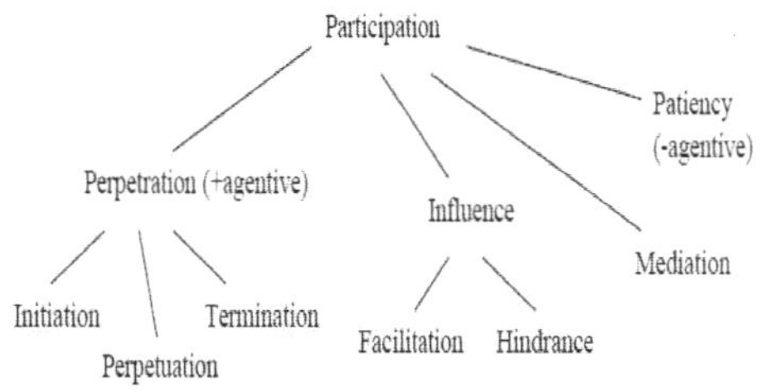

Figure 1. Modes of Participation

Perpetration: A substance perpetrates an action (direct and agentive participation in a process).
Initiation: A substance initiates a process. Example:.

electron transport ← *electron transporter activity* (0.3%/137, 96.4%)

needs to be extended (by drawing on those terms which form part of GO's compositional structure but are not themselves included in GO) by:

electron transport ← *electron transporter*

Perpetuation: A substance sustains a process. Perpetuation normally presupposes that at some earlier time an entity entered into the relation of initiation with the process in question. However, perpetuators are of course not by necessity themselves initiators. Example,

proteolysis and peptidolysis ← *subtilase activity (0.2%/63, 96.8%),*

which again needs to be extended by:

proteolysis and peptidolysis ← *subtilase*

Termination: A substance terminates a process (for example an operator terminates the projection of a film). Termination normally presupposes that there has obtained in the immediately prior interval of time a relation of perpetuation. Processes cannot pass from initiation to termination instantaneously. Example:

mitochondrial membrane	electron transport	carbon-monoxide oxygenase activity	13

In the above example, the association between carbon-monoxide oxygenase and electron transport are that of termination. There is an additional association to the location of this process in the mitochondrial membranes.

Facilitation: A substance plays a secondary role in a process. Example:

protein biosynthesis ← *large ribosomal subunit (0.1%/56, 98.2%)*

Hindrance, prevention: A substance has a negative effect on the unfolding of a process. Example:

DNA transposition ← *transposase activity (1.2%/505, 91.5%).*

While transposase initiates DNA transposition, it also causes an auto-inhibition later.

Mediation: A substance plays an indirect role in the unfolding of a process relating other participants. Example:

formate dehydrogenase complex	electron transport	carbon-monoxide oxygenase activity	18

In this relationship, formate dehydrogenase plays the role of a mediator of electron transport.

Patiency: A substance is being acted on by a process. Example:

provirus	provirus integration	prophage integrase activity	11

In this relationship, provirus is being integrated by the process of provirus integration.

5.1.3 Relations with Signature <SNAP Dependent, SPAN>

Realization: There are three main modes of realization, which result by applying the distinctions dealt with in 5.1.2 (initiation, termination and persistence) but substituting "function" for "activity".

Initiation: *electron transport* ← *electron transporter function*

Termination. *electron transport* ← *carbon-monoxide oxygenase function*

5.1.4 Relations with Signature <SPAN, SNAP>

Relations between Processes and Substances

Creation: A process brings into being a substance. Example:

integral to membrane	steroid biosynthesis	3(or 17)beta-hydroxysteroid dehydrogenase activity	2

As in the previous cases, this association can be extended to:

steroid ← 3(or17)beta-hydroxysteroid dehydrogenase activity

Sustaining in being: A process sustains in being a substance.

membrane	cell growth and/or maintenance	protease inhibitor activity	60

The protease inhibitor activity maintains the membrane structure. Further work needs to be done to understand the granularity of such relations.

Degradation: A process has negative effects upon a substance. Example:

D-amino-acid dehydrogenase complex	amino acid metabolism	lyase activity	2

This relation associates a lyase activity with the degradation of D-amino-acid dehydrogenase complex.

5.1.5 Spatiotemporal projection

Temporal Projection. Processes are directly projectible onto the axis of time. And a substance is indirectly projectible onto a period of time through the mediation of a process in which it is involved. Examples:

Biological process	Molecular function	Weight
acetyl-CoA biosynthesis from pyruvate	dihydrolipoamide dehydrogenase activity	3
acetyl-CoA biosynthesis from pyruvate	dihydrolipoamide S-acetyltransferase activity	5
acetyl-CoA biosynthesis from pyruvate	phosphate acetyltransferase activity	1
acetyl-CoA biosynthesis from pyruvate	pyruvate dehydrogenase (lipoamide) activity	5
acetyl-CoA biosynthesis from pyruvate	pyruvate dehydrogenase activity	5

While we cannot infer such projections directly from a single association rule, we can get a rough approximation if we consider more than one rule together.

Spatial Projection. Processes are projectible also onto the SPAN spatiotemporal regions in which they occur, as also onto the (SNAP) spatial regions where they start and end. Examples:

membrane ← oligopeptide transport; transporter activity (0.1%/44, 100.0%)

ribosome ← ribosome biogenesis; protein biosynthesis (0.2%/88, 93.2%)

6 Discussion

The association rules yielded by our methodology are only the beginning of a process of deciphering the ontological relations across various granularities within the extended GO framework. We need to formally analyse all the rules in order to understand how best they fit within formal ontology and how they can be put together to create larger ontologies within systems biology.

In validating these associations one method is to consider those associations which have been detected on the basis of the annotations present within GO coming from other source databases. Clearly if a rule obtains across a plurality of databases then the corresponding association will be stronger. One disadvantage of this method, however, is that annotations of gene products from different databases to GO are not uniform and so the results cannot be relied upon beyond a certain limit of accuracy. Various other aspects of annotations, for instance, the species under investigation or the pertinent strength of evidence will need to be considered.

A further extension of the work will be to predict "unknown" entities. A large number of annotations is made to the three GO terms *cellular component unknown*, *molecular function unknown* and *biological process unknown*. In those caseswhere there we have association rules without such unknown terms but otherwise relating to the same entities, it could be that the relevant unknown entity will be able to be predicted. This can be done with annotations from a single database source or by putting together annotations from multiple sources. We need to do further work in this area. For example, in the following example, we can establish that in the case where mf is *GTP binding* and cc is *membrane*, the known bf is either *pathogenesis* or *sporulation* (sensu *Bacteria*) or *protein secretion of metabolism*. Thus it is probable that the unknown process here corresponds to one or other of these alternatives.

Cellular component	Biological process	Molecular function
membrane	pathogenesis	GTP binding
membrane	sporulation (sensu Bacteria)	GTP binding
membrane	protein secretion	GTP binding
membrane	metabolism	GTP binding
membrane	biological_process unknown	GTP binding

7 Acknowledgements

Work on this paper was carried out under the auspices of the Wolfgang Paul Program of the Humboldt Foundation and also of the EU Network of Excellence in Semantic Datamining and the project "Forms of Life" sponsored by the Volkswagen Foundation.

References

Agrawal R, Srikant R. Fast algorithms for mining association rules in large databases . *Proc International Conference on Very Large Databases*, Santiage, Chile, (Morgan Kaufmann, 1994) 478-499.

Azuaje FJ, Bodenreider O. Incorporating Ontology-Driven Similarity Knowledge into Functional Genomics: An Exploratory Study. *Proc IEEE Fourth Symposium on Bioinformatics and Bioengineering* 2004. (In press)

Borgelt C, Kruse R. Induction of Association Rules: Apriori Implementation. in: *15th Conference on Computational Statistics* (Compstat 2002, Berlin, Germany) Physica Verlag, Heidelberg, Germany 2002

Burgun A, Bodenreider O, Aubry M, Mosser J. Dependence Relations in Gene Ontology: A Preliminary Study. *Gene Ontology Workshop*, Leipzig, May 2004.

Camon E, Magrane M, Barrell D, Lee V, Dimmer E, Maslen J, Binns D, Harte N, Lopez R, Apweiler R. The Gene Ontology Annotation (GOA) Database: sharing knowledge in Uniprot with Gene Ontology. *Nucleic Acids Res.* 2004 Jan 1;32 Database issue:D262-6.

Clelland S, Oinn T. Comparing protein structure and function: mapping CluSTr into GO and analysis of the results. http://www.ebi.ac.uk/ego/project.pdf?&format=simple

Creighton C, Hanash S. Mining gene expression databases for association rules. *Bioinformatics.* 2003 Jan;19(1):79-86.

Gene Ontology Consortium. Creating the Gene Ontology. *Genome Res.* 2001. 11: 1425-1433.

Kriventseva, E. V., Fleischmann, W., Zdobnov, E. M., Apweiler, R. (2001). CluSTr: a database of clusters of SWISS-PROT+TrEMBL proteins. *Nucleic Acids Res* 29: 33-36

Kumar A, Smith B. Towards a Proteomics Metaclassification. Proc *IEEE Fourth Symposium on Bioinformatics and Bioengineering* 2004. (In press)

Kumar A, Smith B. The Universal Medical Language System and the Gene Ontology: Some Critical Reflections. *Lecture Notes in Computer Science.* 2003 Sep; 2821/2003: 135 – 148.

Mason, O. Automatic Processing of Local Grammar Patterns. Proceedings of the 7th Annual Colloquium for the UK Special Interest Group for Computational Linguistics, University of Birmingham, 6-7th January 2004, p.166-171.

Ogren PV, Cohen KB, Acquaah-Mensah GK, Eberlein J, Hunter L. The Compositional Structure of Gene Ontology Terms. Pacific Symposium on Biocomputing 2004;9:214-225

Pertea G, Huang X, Liang F, Antonescu V, Sultana R, Karamycheva S, Lee Y, White J, Cheung F, Parvizi B, Tsai J, Quackenbush J. TIGR Gene Indices clustering tools (TGICL): a software system for fast clustering of large EST datasets. Bioinformatics. 2003 Mar 22;19(5):651-2.

Resnik P. "Using information content to evaluate semantic similarity in a taxonomy", in Proc. of the *14th International Joint Conference on Artificial Intelligence*, Montreal, pp. 448-453, 1995.

Smith B and Grenon P. The Cornucopia of Formal Relations, forthcoming in DIALECTA

Smith B, Koehler J, Kumar A. On the Application of Formal Principles to Life Science Data: A Case Study in the Gene Ontology. in: Proc DILS 2004. (*Lecture Notes in Bioinformatics* Nr. 2994)

Smith, B., Williams, J., Schulze-Kremer, S.: The Ontology of the Gene Ontology. In: *Proc. Annual Symposium of the American Medical Informatics Association* (2003) 609-613

Thomas PD, Campbell MJ, Kejariwal A, Mi H, Karlak B, Daverman R, Diemer K, Muruganujan A, Narechania A. PANTHER: a library of protein families and subfamilies indexed by function. *Genome Res.* 2003 Sep;13(9):2129-41.

Zhu H, Huang S, Dhar P. The next step in systems biology: simulating the temporospatial dynamics of molecular network. *Bioessays.* 2004 Jan;26(1):68-72.

Discovering Specific Semantic Relationships between Nouns and Verbs in a Specialized French Corpus

Vincent CLAVEAU and **Marie-Claude L'HOMME**
OLST - University of Montreal
C.P. 6128, succ. Centre-Ville
Montréal, QC, H3C 3J7
Canada
{Vincent.Claveau,Marie-Claude.L'Homme}@umontreal.ca

Abstract

Recent literature in computational terminology has shown an increasing interest in identifying various semantic relationships between terms. In this paper, we propose an original strategy to find specific noun-verb combinations in a specialized corpus. We focus on verbs that convey a meaning of realization. To acquire these noun-verb pairs, we use ASARES, a machine learning technique that automatically infers extraction patterns from examples and counter-examples of realization noun-verb pairs. The patterns are then applied to the corpus to retrieve new pairs. Results, measured with a large test set, show that our acquisition technique outperforms classical statistical methods used for collocation acquisition. Moreover, the inferred patterns yield interesting clues on which structures are more likely to convey the target semantic link.

1 Introduction

Recent literature in computational terminology has shown an increasing interest in identifying various semantic relationships between terms. Different strategies have been developed in order to identify pairs of terms that share a specific semantic relationship (such as hyperonymy or meronymy) or to build classes of terms.

However, most strategies are based on "internal" or "external methods" (Grabar and Zweigenbaum, 2002), *i.e.* methods that rely on the form of terms or on the information gathered from contexts. (In some cases, an additional resource, such as a dictionary or a thesaurus, is used during the identification process.) The work reported here infers specific semantic relationships based on sets of examples and counter-examples.

In this paper, the method is applied to a French corpus on computing to find noun-verb combinations in which verbs convey a meaning of realization. The work is carried out in order to assist terminographers in the enrichment of a dictionary on computing that includes collocational information (L'Homme, 2004).

Even though this work is carried out for terminographical and lexicographical purposes, it can certainly be of use in other applications, namely information retrieval. Indeed, such rich semantic links can be used to extend indices or reformulate queries (similar to the work by Voorhees (1994) with WORDNET relations).

2 Objectives

The noun-verb combinations we aim to identify have the following characteristics. They share:

- A syntactic relationship : nouns can be subjects (*e.g.*, "*ordinateur tourne*"; "*computer runs*"); direct objects (*e.g.*, "*configurer l'application*"; "*configure the application*"); or second complement (*e.g.*, "*charger x dans la mémoire*"; "*load x into memory*");
- A valid semantic relationship. The following semantic relationships are sought:
    1. verbs that refer to activities carried out by the nouns (*e.g.*, "*serveur démarre*"; "*server starts*");
    2. verbs that refer to uses of the nouns (*e.g.*, "*activer une option*"; "*activate an option*" or "*naviguer sur Internet*"; "*surf the Internet*");
    3. verbs that refer to activities carried out by means of the nouns (*e.g.*, "*activer l'option au moyen de cette commande*"; "*activate this option with this command*"); and, finally,
    4. verbs that refer to the processes by which nouns are prepared fur use (*e.g.*, "*installer un logiciel*"; "*install an application*").

These noun-verb combinations will hereafter be called *valid N-V pairs*.

The semantic relationships listed above correspond to a set of lexical functions (LFs) defined in (Mel'čuk et al., 1984 1999), *i.e.* LFs used to represent realization (*e.g.*, $Fact_i$, $Real_i$, $Labreal_{ij}$) and to represent the process by which something is prepared ($Prepar$)[1]. (Both of these types of LFs can be combined with others [to create complex lexical functions].) These LFs are opposed to support verbs represented by the LFs $Func_i$, $Oper_i$, $Labor_{ij}$ (*e.g.*, "*créer un fichier*"; "*create a file*"; "*definir une variable*"; "*define a variable*").).

Realization verbs (and verbs denoting the preparation of nouns) were chosen since they are believed to be frequent in technical corpora, such as the corpus of computing used in this experiment. However, this is seen as a first step in order to validate an acquisition process for semantically-related V-N pairs. Other semantic relationships could be sought in the future.

3 Related work

A number of applications have relied on distributional analysis (Harris, 1971) in order to build classes of semantically related terms. This approach, which uses words that appear in the context of terms to formulate hypotheses on their semantic relatedness (Habert et al., 1996, for example), does not specify the relationship itself. Hence, synonyms, co-hyponyms, hyperonyms, *etc.* are not differentiated.

More recent work on terminology structuring has focussed on formal similarity to develop hypotheses on the semantic relationships between terms: Daille (2003) uses derivational morphology; Grabar and Zweigenbaum (2002) use, as a starting point, a number of identical characters.

Up to now, the focus has been on nouns and adjectives, since these structuring methods have been applied to lists of extracted candidate terms (Habert et al., 1996; Daille, 2003) or to lists of admitted terms (Grabar and Zweigenbaum, 2002). As a consequence, relationships considered have been mostly synonymic or taxonomic, or defined as term variations.

On the other hand, other work has been carried out in order to acquire collocations. Most of these endeavours have focused on purely statistical acquisition techniques (Church and Hanks, 1990), on linguisitic acquisition (by the use of Part-of-Speech filters hand-crafted by a linguist) (Oueslati, 1999) or, more frequently, on a combination of the two (Smadja, 1993; Kilgarriff and Tugwell, 2001, for example). It is worth noting that although these techniques are able to identify N-V pairs, they do not specify the relationship between N and V, nor are they capable of focusing on a subset of N-V pairs. The original acquisition methodology we present in the next section will allow us to overcome this limitation.

4 Methodology for finding valid noun-verb pairs

This section is devoted to the description of the methodology and the data we use to acquire semantically related noun-verb pairs. We first describe the specialized corpus used in this experiment. Then, we briefly present ASARES, a pattern inference tool, on which our acquisition strategy relies. Finally, we explain the different steps of the acquisition process.

4.1 Computer science corpus

The French corpus used in our experiments is composed of more than 50 articles from books or web sites specialized in computer science; all of them were published between 1988 and 2003. It covers different computer science sub-domains (networking, managing Unix computers, webcams...) and comprises 600,000 words.

Segmentation, morpho-syntactic tagging and lemmatization have been carried out using the tool CORDIAL[2]. Each word is accompanied by its lemma and Part-of-Speech tag (noun, verb, adjective). Also, the tool indicates inflection (gender and number for nouns, tense and person for verbs) and gives syntactic information (head-modifier) for noun phrases.

4.2 Overview of ASARES

The method used for the acquisition of N-V pairs relies mainly on ASARES, a pattern inference tool. ASARES is presented in detail in (Claveau et al., 2003). We simply give a short account of its basic principles herein.

ASARES is based on a Machine Learning technique, Inductive Logic Programming (ILP) (Muggleton and De-Raedt, 1994), which infers general morpho-syntactic patterns from a set of examples (this set is noted E^+ hereafter) and counter-examples (E^-) of the elements one

[1]However, our interpretation of LFs in this work is much looser, since we admitted verbs that would not be considered to be members of true collocations as Mel'čuk et al. (1984 1999) define them, *i.e.* groups of lexical units that share a restricted cooccurrence relationship.

[2]CORDIAL is a commercial product of Synapse-Développement.

wants to acquire and their context. The contextual patterns produced can then be applied to the corpus in order to retrieve new elements. The acquisition process can be summarized in 3 steps:

1. construction of the sets of examples (and counter-examples);
2. inference of extraction patterns with ASARES; and
3. extraction of N-V pairs from the corpus with the inferred patterns.

ASARES has been previously applied to the acquisition of word pairs sharing semantic relations defined in the Generative Lexicon framework (Pustejovsky, 1995) and called qualia relations (Bouillon et al., 2001). Here, we propose to use ASARES in a quite similar way to retrieve our valid N-V pairs. However, the N-V combinations sought are more specific than those that were identified in these previous experiments.

Formally, ILP aims at inferring logic programs (sets of Horn clauses, noted H) from a set of facts (examples and counter-examples of the concept to be learnt) and background knowledge (B), such that the program H logically entails the examples with respect to the background knowledge and rejects (most of) the counter-examples. This is transcribed by the two logical formulae $B \wedge H \models E^+$, $B \wedge H \not\models E^-$, which set the aim of an ILP algorithm.

In this framework, ASARES infers clauses expressing morpho-syntactic patterns that generalize the structures of sentences containing the target element (examples) but not the structures of the sentences containing counter-examples. The background knowledge encodes information about each word occurring in the example or counter-example, namely the meaning of its tag (*e.g.*, adjective in plural form, infinitive verb).

The main benefits of this acquisition technique lie in the inferred patterns. Indeed, contrary to the more classical statistical methods (Mutual Information, Loglike..., see below) used for collocation acquisition (see (Pearce, 2002) for a review), these patterns allow:

1. understanding of the results, that is, why a specific element has been retrieved or not;
2. highlighting of the corpus-specific structures conveying the target element.

In addition to its explanatory capacity, this symbolic acquisition technique has obtained good results for other acquisition tasks when compared to existing statistical techniques (Bouillon et al., 2002).

4.3 Acquisition process

To infer extraction patterns, ASARES needs a set of examples (E^+) and a set of counter-examples (E^-) of the elements we want to retrieve. In our case, E^+ must thus be composed of (POS-tagged) sentences containing valid N-V pairs; conversely, E^- must be composed of sentences containing non-valid N-V pairs. While this step is tedious and usually carried out manually, the originality of our work lies in the fact that E^+ and E^- are obtained automatically.

To produce the positive examples, we use the existing entries of a terminological database we are currently developing. These entries are thus a kind of *bootstrap* in our acquisition process. More precisely, every N-V pair in which V is defined in the database as a realization verb for N is included. Then, all sentences in our corpus containing this N-V pair are considered as examples and added to E^+. Note that we do not check if each occurrence of the N-V pair actually shares the target semantic link or even a syntactic link in the sentences that are extracted. Some of the examples in E^+ might be incorrect, but ASARES tolerates a certain amount of *noise*.

A totally different technique is needed to produce the E^- set, since no information concerning verbs that are not semantically related is available in the terminological database. To obtain a list of invalid N-V pairs, we acquire them from our corpus using a statistical technique. This produces a list of all N-V pairs that appear in the same sentence, and assigns each a score. Many statistical coefficients exist (Manning and Schütze, 1999); most of them can be easily expressed with the help of a contingency table similar to that reproduced in Table 1 and by noting $S = a + b + c + d$. For example, the

	V_j	V_k, $k \neq j$
N_i	a	b
N_l, $l \neq i$	c	d

Table 1: Contingency table for the pair N_i-V_j

Mutual Information coefficient is defined as:

$$MI = log_2 \frac{a}{(a+b)(a+c)}$$

and the loglike coefficient (Dunning, 1993) as: $Log = a\,log\,a + b\,log\,b + c\,log\,c + d\,log\,d - (a +$

$b)\,log(a+b) - (a+c)\,log(a+c) - (b+d)\,log(b+d) - (c+d)\,log(c+d) + S\,log\,S$.
In the work presented here, we have adopted the Loglike coefficient. From the N-V pair list produced with this method, we have chosen the pairs that obtained the lower Loglike scores. As for the positive examples, we consider that each sentence containing one of the pairs is a counter-example and is added to E^-.

Finally, ASARES is launched with these E^+ and E^- sets; each containing about 2600 sentences. About 80 patterns are then produced; some of them are presented and discussed in section 5.1. These patterns can now be applied to the corpus in order to retrieve valid N-V pairs.

5 Performance evaluation

5.1 Inferred patterns

The inferred patterns give some interesting information about the way the target semantic relationships are expressed in our corpus. While some structures are general, others seem very specific to our corpus.

First of all, proximity is an important factor in valid relationships between nouns and verbs; it can be observed in numerous patterns. For example, the inferred Horn clause:
realization(N,V) :- common_noun(N), contiguous(N,V), N≠V. transcribes the fact that a noun and a verb may be a valid N-V pair if N is a common noun (common_noun(N)) and V is contiguous to N (contiguous(N,V). (Determiners are not taken into account.) This pattern covers the case in which N precedes V, such as "*les utilisateurs lancent tour-à-tour leurs programmes*" ("*users launch in turn their programs*") or in which V precedes N, such as "*il est donc nécessaire d'exécuter la commande* `depmod`" ("*thus, it is necessary to run the* `depmod` *command*". A quite similar clue is given in the following pattern:
realization(N,V) :- near_verb(N,V), suc(V,C), suc(C,N), noun(N), V≠C, N≠C, N≠V. The near_verb(N,V) predicate means that no verb occurs between N and V, and suc(X,Y) that the word X is followed by Y. This clause can be expressed in a more classical way as *V + (anything but a verb) + N* and retrieves pairs like "*C'est un service qui vous permet de vous connecter à Internet*" ("*This is a service that allows you to connect to the Internet*").

Another frequent clue in the patterns produced is, unsurprisingly, that N must be the head of a noun phrase. For example, realization(N,V) :- near_word(N,V), near_verb(N,V), precedes(V,N), noun_ph_head(N), pred(N,C), preposition(C), V≠C, N≠C, N≠V. This pattern means *V + (anything but a verb)? + (preposition) + N head of a noun phrase* and retrieves pairs such as: "*les dispositifs d'impression n'étaient pas contrôlés par ordinateur*" ("*the printing devices were not controlled by computer*").

Prepositions also play an important part and appear frequently in the patterns: realization(N,V) :- near_verb(N,V), pred(N,C), lemma(C,"sur"), V≠C, N≠C, N≠V. (that is *V + (anything but a verb)* + sur + N*) covers for example "*un terminal (...) permet de travailler sur l'ordinateur*" ("*a terminal (...) allows [one/the user] to work on the computer*").

The pattern realization realization(N,V) :- near_verb(N,V), precedes(V,N), pred(N,C), lemma(C,"à"), V≠C, N≠C, N≠V., that is *V + (anything but a verb)* + à + N*, covers "*comment vous connecter à Internet*" ("*How to connect to the Internet*").

realization(N,V) :- near_verb(N,V), precedes(N,V), pred(V,C), lemma(C,"à"), common_noun(N), V≠C, N≠C, N≠V., that is *N + (anything but a verb)* + à + V*, covers "*(...) mode de traitement des données suivant lequel les programmes à exécuter (...)*" ("*...mode of data processing in which the programs to execute...*").

A certain number of patterns express structures more specific to our corpus. For example, the clause:
realization(N,V) :- near_verb(N,V), precedes(V,N), suc(N,C), proper_noun(C), common_noun(N), V≠C, N≠C, N≠V. (that is, *V + (anything but a verb)* + common noun N + (proper noun)*) is very specific to structures including a proper noun, such as the sentence: "*(...) Internet utilise le protocole TCP/IP (...)*" ("*the Internet uses the TCP/IP protocol*").

5.2 Methodology for evaluation

In order to evaluate the quality of the extracted N-V pairs, we are interested in two different measures. The first one expresses the completeness of the set of retrieved N-V pairs, that is, how many valid pairs are found with respect to the total number of pairs which should have been found; this is the recall rate. The second measure indicates the reliability of the set of retrieved N-V pairs, that is, how many valid pairs are found with respect to the total number of retrieved pairs; this is the precision rate (defined below). These two rates were evaluated using a test sample containing all this information.

To construct this test set, we have focused our attention on ten domain-specific terms: *commande* (*command*), *configuration*, *fichier* (*file*), *Internet*, *logiciel* (*software*), *option*, *ordinateur* (*computer*), *serveur* (*server*), *système* (*system*), *utilisateur* (*user*). The terms have been identified as the most specific to our corpus by a program developed by Drouin (2003) and called TERMOSTAT. The ten most specific nouns have been produced by comparing our corpus of computing to the French corpus *Le Monde*, composed of newspaper articles (Lemay et al., 2004). Note that to prevent any bias in the results, none of these terms were used as positive examples during the pattern inference step. (They were removed from the example set.)

For each of these 10 nouns, a manual identification of valid and invalid pairs was carried out. Linguists were asked to analyze the sentences and decide whether the highlighted pairs were valid N-V pairs. Examples of the sentences produced are given in Table 2 for the term *utilisateur* (*user*). A pair is considered as valid if at least one of its occurrences has the desired semantic (and syntactic) relationship (*cf.* section 2).

Finally, 603 of the N-V pairs examined are valid and 4446 are considered not to be valid. The results for each noun are detailed in Table 3.

	valid	non-valid	total
commande	114	346	460
configuration	4	361	365
fichier	21	604	625
option	69	324	393
système	82	605	687
Internet	9	535	544
ordinateur	85	432	517
utilisateur	96	435	531
logiciel	64	440	504
serveur	59	364	423
Total	603	4446	5049

Table 3: Summary of the test set

5.3 Results

To compare the results obtained by our technique with the analysis carried out manually, we use the traditional precision/recall approach. Thus we applied the patterns to the corpus and kept all the pairs retrieved when N is one of the ten specific nouns. The results of the comparison are summarized with the help of confusion matrices like the one presented in Table 4[3].

	actual valid	actual non-valid	Total
predicated valid	TP	FP	PrP
predicated non-valid	FN	TN	PrN
Total	AP	AN	S

Table 4: Confusion matrix

It is important to note here that the values in this confusion matrix depend on a parameter: a detection threshold. Indeed, a single occurrence of a N-V pair with the patterns is not sufficient for a pair to be considered as valid. The threshold, called s, represents the minimal number of occurrences to be detected to consider a pair as valid. The recall and precision rates (respectively R and P), measured on our test set, are thus defined according to s.

In order to represent every possible value of R and P according to s, we draw a recall-precision graph in which each value of P is related to its corresponding value of R. Figure 1 gives the graph obtained when applying the inferred patterns to the test set. For comparison purposes, Figure 1 also indicates the recall-precision graphs obtained by two common statistical techniques for collocation acquisition (the Loglike et Mutual Information coefficients presented in section 4.3). As a baseline, this graph also gives the density, computed as AP/S, which represents the precision that would be obtained by a system deciding randomly if a pair is valid or not.

The recall-precision graph shows that our symbolic technique outperforms the two statistical ones; for a fixed recall, the precision gain is up to 45% with respect to the Loglike results and is even higher with respect the MI coefficient. Thus, our acquisition technique meets the objective of offering assistance to the terminographer, since it provides many reliable N-V pair candidates. However, results show that invalid pairs are also retrieved; thus a manual analysis remains unavoidable.

5.4 Discussion of the results

When examining the retrieved pairs, it appears that most invalid N-V pairs can be classified in

[3]The meaning of the variables is given by the combination of the letters: A means actual, Pr predicated, T true, F false, P positive and N negative.

Examples	**Comment**
`utilisateur___exécuter 162.823 13.907792621292` `* MemCheckBoxInRunDlg Autorise les utilisateurs#N# à exécuter#V# un programme 16 bits dans un processus VDM ( Virtual DOS Machine ) dédié ( non partagé ) .`	Valid syntactic and semantic relationship: "user runs a program"
`utilisateur___formater 162.823 0.27168791461736` `* AllocateDasd Détermine quels utilisateurs#N# peuvent formater#V# et éjecter les disques_durs amovibles .`	Valid syntactic and semantic relationship: "user formats a hard disk"
`utilisateur___lancer 162.823 17.9010990569368` `* Il utilise donc le numéro de l_ utilisateur#N# réel qui a lancé#V# la commande pour savoir si c_ est bien l_ utilisateur#N# root qui l_ a lancé#V# .`	Valid syntactic and semantic relationship: "user launches a command"
Counter-examples	**Comment**
`utilisateur___accepter 162.823 0.0059043737128377` `* Ces commandes sont absolument essentielles pour pouvoir utiliser le système , mais elles sont assez rébarbatives et peu_d_ utilisateurs#N# acceptent#V# de s_ en contenter .`	Syntactic relationship is valid; Semantic relationship is not valid
`utilisateur___entourer 162.823 0.41335402801632` `* Mais , côté utilisateur#N# , plus on a entouré#V# ou rempli son Macintosh de périphériques , plus grands sont les risques de rencontrer des blocages ou des sautes_d_humeur .`	Syntactic relationship is not valid

Table 2: Positive and negative examples with *utilisateur* (Engl. *user*)

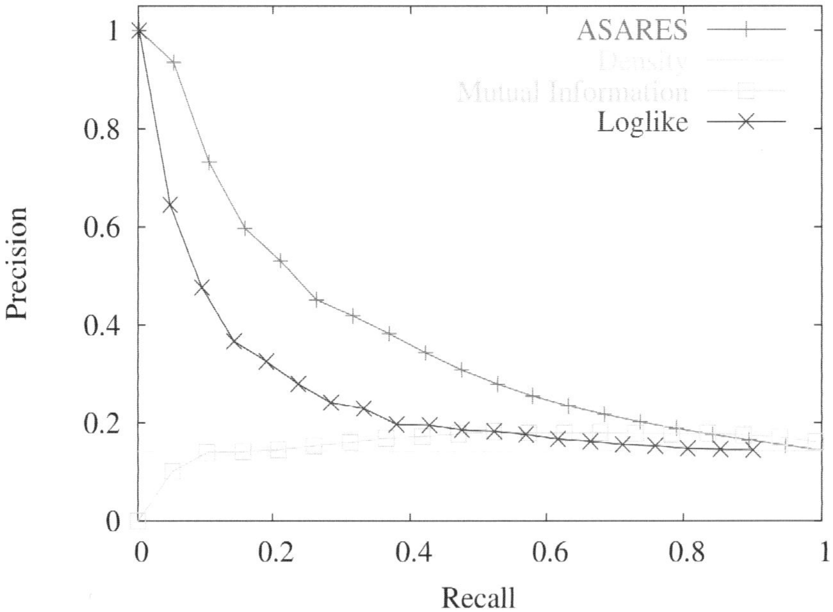

Figure 1: Recall-Precision graph

one of the four following categories.

First, some errors are due to tagging mistakes. For example, in the sentence "*la première solution est d'utiliser la commande* **`date`**" ("*the first solution is to use the* **`date`** *command*") the noun **`date`** was incorrectly tagged as a verb, and the N-V pair *commande-dater* was retrieved by one of the inferred patterns. Even if this kind of error does not come directly from our acquisition technique and does not call into question our approach, it is still a factor that should be taken into account, especially when considering the choice of the tagger and the quality of the texts composing our corpus.

Secondly, in a few cases, there is no syntactic link between N and V, as is the case with *logiciel-garantir* (*software-guarantee*) in "*cette phase garantit la vérification du logiciel*" ("*this step guarantees the software verification*"). Even if these errors are rare in the retrieved pairs examined, our symbolic extraction system could certainly be enhanced with information about the syntactic function of nouns (subject, direct object...). The learning algorithm could then incorporate this information and produce more relevant patterns.

Thirdly, some N-V pairs are retrieved, although there is no semantic link between N and V, or at least, not a semantic link that would be encoded by a terminographer in a dictionary. This is the case for *ordinateur-savoir* (*computer-know*) in "*l'ordinateur ne sait pas où chercher*" ("*the computer does not know where to look*"). Again, morpho-syntactic information is not always sufficient to distinguish between semantically related pairs and non-semantically (but syntactically) related ones.

Finally, other very frequent errors are caused by the fact that there actually is an interesting semantic link between N and V in a retrieved pair, but not the realization link we are looking for. Indeed, some nouns belonging to specific semantic classes will often cooccur with verbs expressing realization meanings (and thus often appear in valid N-V pairs) while others do not. For example, nouns like *ordinateur* (*computer*) and *utilisateur* (*user*) often appear in valid N-V pairs. On the other hand, other nouns clearly do not appear in combinations with realization verbs (*e.g.*, *configuration*; *Internet*, refer to Table 3).

These last two kinds of error clearly illustrate the limitations of our symbolic approach (but are also very frequent errors in statistical approaches since cooccurrence is not enough to capture subtle semantic distinctions). In fact, they tend to show that our method could be enhanced if it could incorporate richer linguistic information. Indeed, morpho-syntactic information is not always sufficient to operate fine-grained sense distinctions. For example, the two sentences below have the same combination of Part-of-Speech tags: "*vous pouvez <u>utiliser</u> la <u>commande</u> exit*" ("*you can use the exit command*") and "*vous devez <u>choisir</u> l'<u>option</u> 64MB*" ("*you must choose the 64MB option*"); in the first one the underlined N-V pair is valid whereas this is not the case in the second one. Realization verbs for *option* would be *valider* (*validate*) and *activer* (*activate*), for example. Here again, these subtle distinctions could be handled by our symbolic method provided that some semantic information is given on nouns This could be supplied by a semantic tagger.

6 Concluding remarks and future work

We have presented an original acquisition process for noun-verb pairs in which verbs convey a realization meaning. These noun-verb pairs are acquired from a domain-specific corpus of computing. Our acquisition method, which relies on ASARES, a extraction pattern inference technique, produces results that are quite good and could improve manual terminographical work. In particular, our method outperforms classical statistical techniques often used for collocation acquisition. Moreover, the inferred patterns give interesting clues about the structures that are likely to convey the target semantic link.

Many possibilities for future work are suggested by this experiment. Concerning our acquisition process, some adaptations could certainly improve the results, currently limited by the sole use of Part-of-Speech tags and noun-phrase information. As was previously mentioned, syntactic and semantic information could be added to the corpus through a tagging and parsing process. These two enrichments could help to overcome some limitations of our symbolic approach to capture the nature of N-V relationships. In terms of applications, it would be interesting to use a similar technique for the acquisition of other more specific semantic links between nouns and verbs and even between nouns and nouns or other categories of words. These semantic relationships would allow us to complete the description of the terminological units contained in our dictionary of computing. The comparison of the acquisition results and of the inferred patterns could lead to interesting insights.

Aknowlegements

The authors would like to thank Sahara Iveth Carreño Cruz and Léonie Demers-Dion for their help in analyzing the data and Elizabeth Marshman for her comments on a previous version of this paper.

References

Pierrette Bouillon, Vincent Claveau, Cécile Fabre, and Pascale Sébillot. 2001. Using Part-of-Speech and Semantic Tagging for the Corpus-Based Learning of Qualia Structure Elements. In *First International Workshop on Generative Approaches to the Lexicon, GL'2001*, Geneva, Switzerland.

Pierrette Bouillon, Vincent Claveau, Cécile Fabre, and Pascale Sébillot. 2002. Acquisition of Qualia Elements from Corpora – Evaluation of a Symbolic Learning Method. In *3rd International Conference on Language Resources and Evaluation, LREC 02*, Las Palmas de Gran Canaria, Spain.

Kenneth W. Church and Patrick Hanks. 1990. Word Association Norms, Mutual Information, and Lexicography. *Computational Linguistics*, 16(1):22–29.

Vincent Claveau, Pascale Sébillot, Cécile Fabre, and Pierrette Bouillon. 2003. Learning Semantic Lexicons from a Part-of-Speech and Semantically Tagged Corpus using Inductive Logic Programming. *Journal of Machine Learning Research, special issue on ILP*, 4:493–525.

Béatrice Daille. 2003. Conceptual structuring through term variation. In *Workshop on Multiword Expressions. Analysis, Acquisition and Treatment. Proceedings of the ACL'03*, Sapporo, Japan.

Patrick Drouin. 2003. Term-extraction using non-technical corpora as a point of leverage. *Terminology*, 9(1):99–115.

Ted E. Dunning. 1993. Accurate methods for the statistics of surprise and coincidence. *Computational Linguistics*, 19(1):61–74.

Natalia Grabar and Pierre Zweigenbaum. 2002. Lexically-based terminology structuring. some inherent limits. In *Second Workshop on Computational Terminology, Computerm 2002. Coling 2002*, Taipei, Taiwan.

Benoît Habert, Ellie Naulleau, and Adeline Nazarenko. 1996. Symbolic word clustering for medium-sized corpora. In *Proceedings of the 16th Conference on Computational Linguistics, Coling'96*, Copenhagen, Denmark.

Zellig Harris. 1971. *Structures mathématiques du langage*. Paris: Dunod.

Adam Kilgarriff and David Tugwell. 2001. WORD-SKETCH: Extraction and Display of Significant Collocations for Lexicography. In *Workshop on Collocation: Computational Extraction, Analysis and Exploitation, 39th ACL and 10th EACL Conference*, Toulouse, France.

Chantal Lemay, Marie-Claude L'Homme, and Patrick Drouin. 2004. Two methods for extracting "specific" single-word terms from specialized corpora. Forthcoming.

Marie-Claude L'Homme. 2004. Sélection de termes dans un dictionnaire d'informatique : Comparaison de corpus et critères lexico-sémantiques. In *Euralex 2004. Proceedings*, Lorient, France. Forthcoming.

Christopher D. Manning and Hinrich Schütze. 1999. *Foundations of Statistical Natural Language Processing*. The MIT Press, Cambridge, MA, USA.

Igor Mel'čuk, Nadia Arbatchewsky-Jumarie, Léo Elnitsky, Lidija Iordanskaja, Adèle Lessard, Louise Dagenais, Marie-Noëlle Lefebvre, Suzanne Mantha, and Alain Polguère. 1984–1999. *Dictionnaire explicatif et combinatoire du français contemporain, Recherches lexico-sémantiques*, volumes I-IV. Les Presses de l'Université de Montréal, Montréal, QC, Canada.

Stephen Muggleton and Luc De-Raedt. 1994. Inductive Logic Programming: Theory and Methods. *Journal of Logic Programming*, 19-20:629–679.

Rochdi Oueslati. 1999. *Aide à l'acquisition de connaissances à partir de corpus*. Ph.D. thesis, Univesité Louis Pasteur, Strasbourg, France.

Darren Pearce. 2002. A Comparative Evaluation of Collocation Extraction Techniques. In *3rd International Conference on Language Resources and Evaluation, LREC 02*, Las Palmas de Gran Canaria, Spain.

James Pustejovsky. 1995. *The Generative Lexicon*. The MIT Press, Cambridge, MA, USA.

Frank Smadja. 1993. Retrieving Collocations from Text: XTRACT. *Computational Linguistics*, 19(1):143–178.

Ellen M. Voorhees. 1994. Query Expansion Using Lexical-Semantic Relations. In *Proceedings of ACM SIGIR'94*, Dublin, Ireland.

Automatically Inducing Ontologies from Corpora

Inderjeet Mani

Department of Linguistics
Georgetown University, ICC 452
37th and O Sts, NW
Washington, DC 20057, USA
im5@georgetown.edu

Ken Samuel, Kris Concepcion and David Vogel

The MITRE Corporation
7515 Colshire Drive
McLean, VA 22102, USA
{samuel, kjc9, dvogel}@mitre.org

Abstract

The emergence of vast quantities of on-line information has raised the importance of methods for automatic cataloguing of information in a variety of domains, including electronic commerce and bioinformatics. Ontologies can play a critical role in such cataloguing. In this paper, we describe a system that automatically induces an ontology from any large on-line text collection in a specific domain. The ontology that is induced consists of domain concepts, related by *kind-of* and *part-of* links. To achieve domain-independence, we use a combination of relatively shallow methods along with any available repositories of applicable background knowledge. We describe our evaluation experiences using these methods, and provide examples of induced structures.

1 Introduction

The emergence of vast quantities of on-line information has raised the importance of methods for automatic cataloguing of information in a variety of domains, including electronic commerce and bioinformatics. Ontologies[1] can play a critical role in such cataloguing. In bioinformatics, for example, there is growing recognition that common ontologies, e.g., the Gene Ontology[2], are critical to interoperation and integration of biological data, including both structured data as found in protein databases, as well as unstructured data, as found in on-line biomedical literature.

Constructing an ontology is an extremely laborious effort. Even with some reuse of "core" knowledge from an Upper Model (Cohen et al. 1999), the task of creating an ontology for a particular domain and task has a high cost, incurred for each new domain. Tools that could automate, or semi-automate, the construction of ontologies for different domains could dramatically reduce the knowledge creation cost.

One approach to developing such tools is to rely on information implicit in collections of on-line text in a particular domain. If it were possible to automatically extract terms and their semantic relations from the text corpus, the ontology developer could build on that knowledge, revising it, as needed, etc. This would be more cost-effective than having a human develop the ontology from scratch.

Our approach is inspired by research on topic-focused multi-document summarization of large text collections, where there is a need to characterize the collection content succinctly in a hierarchy of topic terms and their relationships. Current approaches to multi-document summarization combine linguistic analysis, corpus statistics, and the use of background semantic knowledge from generic thesauri such as WordNet to infer semantic information about a person. In extending such approaches to ontology induction, the hypothesis is that similar hybrid approaches can be used to identify technical terms in a domain-specific corpus and infer semantic relationships among them.

In this paper, we describe a system that automatically induces an ontology from any large on-line text collection in a specific domain, to support cataloguing in information access and data integration tasks. The induced ontology consists of domain concepts related by *kind-of* and *part-of* links, but does not include more specialized relations or axioms. The structure of the ontology is a directed acyclic graph (DAG). To achieve domain-independence, we use a combination of relatively shallow methods along with existing repositories of applicable background knowledge. These are described in Section 2. In Section 3, we also introduce a new metric *Relation Precision* for evaluating induced ontologies in comparison with reference ontologies. We have applied our system to produce ontologies in numerous domains:

[1] This research was supported by the National Science Foundation (ITR-0205470).

[2] www.geneontology.org

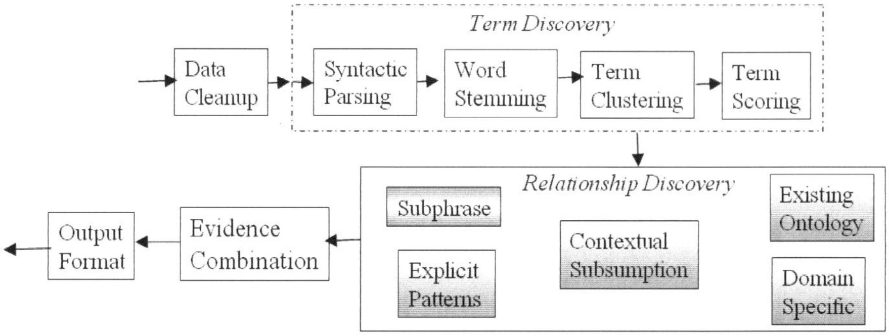

Figure 1: System Architecture

IRS Publication 17	285 k_1	0	285 n_1
Reuters Corpus	9 k_2	19,024	19,043 n_2
Total	294	19,024	19,328

Table 1: Distribution of 'income tax' in domain and background corpora

(i) newswire from the TREC collection (ii) taxation information from the IRS (Publication 17, from (IRS 2001)), (iii) epidemiological newsgroup messages from the Program for Monitoring Emerging Diseases (PROMED) from the Federation of American Scientists[3], (iv) the text of a book by the first author called *Automatic Summarization*, and (v) MEDLINE biomedical abstracts retrieved from the National Library of Medicine's PubMed system[4]. In the latter domain, we have begun building a large ontology using the ontology induction methods along with post-editing by domain experts in molecular biology at Georgetown University[5]. This ontology, called PRONTO, involves hundreds of thousands of protein names found in MEDLINE abstracts and in UNIPROT, the world's largest protein database[6]. It is therefore infeasible to construct PRONTO by hand from scratch. PRONTO is also much larger than other ontologies in the biology area; for example, the Gene Ontology is rather high-level, and contains (as of March 2004) only about 17,000 terms.

2 Approach

2.1 System Architecture

An overall architecture for domain-independent ontology induction is shown in Figure 1. The documents are preprocessed to separate out headers. Next, terms are extracted using finite-state syntactic parsing and scored to discover domain-relevant terms. The subsequent processing infers semantic relations between pairs of terms using the 'weak' knowledge sources run in the order described below. Evidence from multiple knowledge sources is then combined to infer the resulting relations. The resulting ontologies are written out in a standard XML-based format (e.g., XOL, RDF, OWL), for use in various information access applications.

While the ontology induction procedure does not involve human labor, except for writing the preprocessing and term tokenization program for specialized technical domains, the human may edit the resulting ontology for use in a given application. An ontology editor has been developed, discussed briefly in Section 3.1.

2.2 Term Discovery

The system takes a collection of documents in a subject area, and identifies terms characteristic of the domain. In a given domain such as

[3] www.fas.org/promed/

[4] www4.ncbi.nlm.nih.gov/PubMed/

[5] complingone.georgetown.edu/~prot/

[6] pir.georgetown.edu

bioinformatics, specialized term tokenization (into single- and multi-word terms) is required. The protein names can be long, e.g., "steroid/thyroid/retinoic nuclear hormone receptor homolog nhr-35", and involve specialized patterns. In constructing PRONTO, we have used a protein name tagger based on an ensemble of statistical classifiers to tag protein names in collections of MEDLINE abstracts (Anon 2004). Thus, in such a domain, a specialized tagger replaces the components in the dotted box in Figure 1.

In other domains, we adopt a generic term-discovery approach. Here the text is tagged for part-of-speech, and single- and multi-word terms consisting of minimal NPs are extracted using finite-state parsing with CASS (Abney 1996). All punctuation except for hyphens are removed from the terms, which are then lower-cased. Each word in each term is stemmed, with statistics (see below) being gathered for each stemmed term. Multi-word terms are clustered so that open, closed and hyphenated compounds are treated as equivalent, with the most frequent term in the collection being used as the cluster representative.

The terms are scored for domain-relevance based on the assumption that if a term occurs significantly more in a domain corpus than in a more diffuse background corpus, then the term is clearly domain relevant.

As an illustration, in Table 1 we compare the number of documents containing the term 'income tax' (or 'income taxes') in a long (2.18 Mb) IRS publication, Publication 17, from an IRS web site (IRS 2001) compared to a larger (27.63 Mb subset of the) Reuters 21578 news corpus[7]. One would expect that 'income tax' is much more a characteristic of the IRS publication, and this is borne out by the document frequencies in the table. We use the log likelihood ratio (LLR) (Dunning 1993) given by

$$-2\log_2(H_o(p;k_1,n_1,k_2,n_2)/H_a(p_1,p_2;n_1,k_1,n_2,k_2))$$

LLR measures the extent to which a hypothesized model of the distribution of cell counts, H_a, differs from the null hypothesis, H_o (namely, that the percentage of documents containing this term is the same in both corpora). We used a binomial model for H_o and H_a[8].

2.3 Relationship Discovery

The main innovation in our approach is to fuse together information from multiple knowledge sources as evidence for particular semantic relationships between terms. To infer semantic relations such as *kind-of* and *part-of*, the system uses a bottom-up data-driven approach using a combination of evidence from shallow methods.

2.3.1 Subphrase Relations

These are based on the presence of common syntactic heads, and allow us to infer, for example, that 'p68 protein' is a *kind-of* 'protein'. Likewise, in the TREC domain, subphrase analysis tells us that 'electric car' is a kind of 'car', and in the IRS domain, that 'federal income tax' is a kind of 'income tax'.

2.3.2 Existing Ontology Relations

These are obtained from a thesaurus. For example, the Gene Ontology can be used to infer that 'ATP-dependent RNA helicase' is a *kind of* 'RNA-helicase'. Likewise, in the TREC domain, using WordNet tells us that 'tailpipe' is *part of* 'automobile', and in the IRS domain, that 'spouse' is a *kind of* 'person'. Synonyms are also merged together at this stage.

2.3.3 Contextual Subsumption Relations

We also infer hierarchical relations between terms, by top-down clustering using a context-based subsumption (CBS) algorithm. The algorithm uses a probabilistic measure of set covering to find subsumption relations. For each term in the corpus, we note the set of contexts in which the term appears. Term1 is said to subsume term2 when the conditional probability of term1 appearing in a context given the presence of term2, i.e., P(term1|term2), is greater than some threshold.

CBS is based on the algorithm of (Lawrie et al. 2001), which used a greedy approximation of the Domination Set Problem for graphs to discover subsumption relations among terms. Unlike their work, we did not seek to minimize the set of covering terms; therefore, a subsumed term may have multiple parents. The conditional probability threshold (0.8) we use to determine subsumption is much higher than in their approach. We also restrict the height of the hierarchies we build to three tiers. Tightening these latter two constraints appears to notably improve the quality of our subsumption relations.

The largest corpus against which CBS has run is the ProMed corpus where, considering each paragraph a distinct context, there were 117,690 contexts in the 11,198 documents. Here is an example from ProMed of a transitive relation that spans three tiers: 'mosquito' is a hypernym of 'mosquito pool', and 'mosquito' is also a hypernym of 'standing water'.

---

[7] In Publication 17, each "chapter" is a document.

[8] From Table 1, p=294/19238=.015, p_1=285/285=1.0, p_2=9/19043=4.72, k_1=285, n_1=285, k_2=9, n_2=19043.

2.3.4 Explicit Patterns Relations

This knowledge source infers specific relations between terms based on characteristic *cue-phrases* which relate them. For example, the cue-phrase "such as" (Hearst 1992) (Caraballo 1999) suggest a *kind-of* relation, e.g., 'a ligand such as triethylphosphine' tells us that 'triethylphosphene' is a kind of 'ligand'. Likewise, in the TREC domain, 'air toxics such as benzene' can suggest that 'benzene' is a *kind of* 'air toxic'. However, since such cue-phrase patterns tend to be sparse in occurrence, we do not use them in the evaluations described below.

2.3.5 Domain-Specific Knowledge Sources

Although our approach is domain-independent, it is possible to factor in domain knowledge sources for a given domain. For example, in biology, 'ase' is usually a suffix indicating an enzyme. Postmodifying PPs (found using a CASS grammar) can also be useful in some domains, as shown in 'tax on investment income of child' in Figure 2. We have so far, however, not investigated other domain-specific knowledge sources.

2.4 Evidence Combination

The main point about these and other knowledge sources is that each may provide only partial information. Combining these knowledge sources together, we expect, will lead to superior performance compared to just any one of them. Not only do inferences from different knowledge sources support each other, but they are also combined to produce new inferences by transitivity relations. For example, since phrase analysis tells us that 'pyridine metabolism' is a *kind-of* 'metabolism', and Gene Ontology tells us that 'metabolism' is a *kind-of* 'biological process', it follows that 'pyridine metabolism' is a *kind-of* 'biological process'. The evidence combination, in addition to computing transitive closure of these relations, also detects inconsistencies, querying the user to resolve them when detected.

3 Evaluation

3.1 Informal Assessment

Subphrase Relations is a relatively high-precision knowledge source compared to the others, producing many linked chains. Its performance can be improved by flagging and excluding proper names and idioms from its input (e..g, so that 'palm pilot' doesn't show up as a kind-of 'pilot'). However, a chain of such relations can be interrupted by terms that aren't lexically similar, but that are nevertheless in a kind-of relation. Some of these gaps are filled by transitivity relations involving other knowledge sources, especially Existing Ontologies, which is especially useful in filling gaps in some of the upper levels of the ontology. While Contextual Subsumption is good at discovering associations between 'leaves' in the DAG and other concepts, the method cannot reliably infer the label of the relation. For example, in the IRS domain, we obtain 'divorce' as more general than 'decree of divorce' and 'separate maintenance', but we don't know the nature of the relations. Contextual Subsumption-inferred links are directed edges with label 'unknown'.

Overall, the ontologies produced are noisy and require human correction, and the methods can produce many fragments that need to be linked by hand. While the system can detect cycles that need resolution by the human, these rarely arise

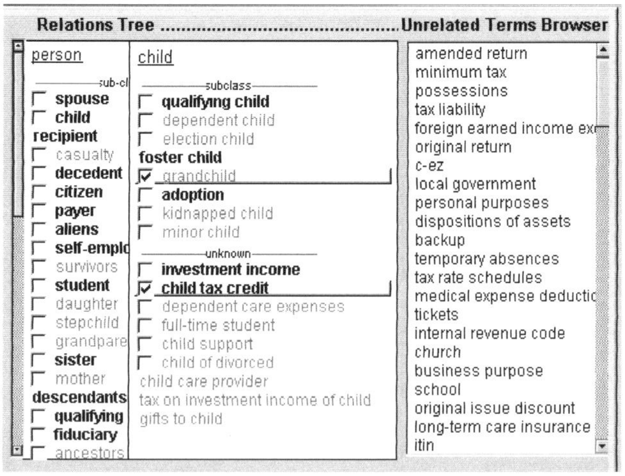

Figure 2: An IRS Ontology viewed in the Ontology Editor

Term	Target DF	Back-ground DF	LLR	IG	MI	DF	TF	TF * IDF
electric	80	61	99.9	99.9	81.3	99.9	99.9	27.8
car	77	56	99.6	99.3	81.5	99.8	99.9	79.4
battery	54	16	99.0	98.2	86.9	98.7	99.9	94.9
emission	15	0	96.5	96.8	99.2	79.1	96.6	64.8
year	58	505	67.9	67.6	25.0	99.2	99.7	65.7
informal	10	29	66.2	66.3	0.2	48.6	99.7	99.2
record	8	138	15.2	15.7	4.4	50.2	99.9	99.9
osha	1	0	0.0	0.0	0.0	0.0	99.9	0.0

Table 2: Comparing Topic 230 Term Percentile Rankings

For a flavor of the kind of results we get, see Figure 2, which displays an ontology induced without any human intervention from IRS Publication 17. Here the DAG is displayed as a tree. The immediate children of 'person', a node high in the ontology, is shown in the left part of the window. Selecting 'child' brings up its kinds as well as some other children linked by "unknown" label via Contextual Subsumption, e.g., 'full-time student'. A list of orphaned terms that aren't related to any others are shown on the far right. The terms with checkboxes are those that occur in the corpus; the others are those that are found exclusively by Existing Ontology Relations. Checking a term allows it to be inspected in its occurrence context in the corpus. The editor comes with a variety of tools to help integrate ontology fragments.

3.2 Human Evaluation

3.2.1 Term Scoring

To evaluate term scoring, we used a corpus of news articles about automobiles that consisted of 85 documents relevant to the TREC Topic 230 query: "Is the automobile industry making an honest effort to develop and produce an electric-powered automobile?" In Table 2, we provide some examples of how the LLR term scoring statistic performed with respect to five others on selected unigrams in the Topic 230 domain: term frequency, document frequency, term frequency times inverse document frequency (TF*IDF), pointwise mutual information (MI), and information gain (IG). Terms in bold are ones we judged important in the Topic 230 domain, the others are deemed unimportant. The numbers are percentile rankings. LLR and IG do equally well, outperforming the others.

We carried out other comparisons for two other domains. In the income-tax domain, a hand-built term list from the IRS contained 82 terms which occurred in IRS Publication 17, of which the system discovered 77 (94% recall). In the ProMed domain, a pre-existing hand-built taxonomy produced by a bioterrorism analyst had 1048 terms which occurred in the ProMed message corpus, of which 607 were discovered by the system (58% recall). However, the hand-built taxonomy, which was built without consulting a corpus, wasn't a full-fledged ontology, for example, there was no label for the parent-child relation.

3.2.2 Term Relationships

We also carried out an evaluation experiment to determine if the relations being discovered by the machine were in keeping with human judgments. We focused here on an evaluation of pairs of knowledge sources. Our experiment examined the case where the system discovered a *kind-of* relation. Here each subject was first asked to read four newspaper articles from the TREC topic-230 sub-collection. The articles were then kept accessible to the subject in a browser window for the subject to consult if needed in answering subsequent questions. The subject was asked to judge, based on the documents read, whether term X was a kind of term Y, term Y was a kind of term X, or neither; e.g., "Is *acid* a kind of *pollutant*, or is *pollutant* a kind of *acid*, or neither?". The subject had one of three mutually exclusive choices; the first two choices were presented in randomized order.

The subjects were 16 native speakers of English unconnected with the project. Each subject was given ten questions to answer in each of the experiments. For each set of ten questions, five were chosen at random from pairs of terms related by (immediate) *kind-of* relations. The remaining five questions were chosen at random from pairs of terms between which the system found no relation whatsoever.

	Human	
System	*kind-of(A, B)*	*not kind-of(A,B)*
kind-of(A, B)	56	18
not kind-of(A,B)	6	74

Table 3: Is X a kind-of Y?

We first discuss inter-subject agreement. Three subjects given the same relation to judge agreed 75% of the time, leading to a Kappa score of 0.72, indicating a good level of agreement. This means that subjects were able to reliably make judgments as to whether A is a *kind of* B in some document.

The results for the 16 subjects are shown in Table 3. When the system is compared to the human as ground truth, this gives a Precision of .90, a Recall of .75, and an F-measure of .82. This performance is also significantly better than random assignment: with chi-square=74.29, with $p < 0.001$[9]. The substantial effect sizes of the chi-square indicates a very solid result. There were 62 decisions involving Subphrase Relations (with 44 True Positives and 18 False Negatives), and 10 decisions involving WordNet (with 12 True Positives). This shows that there is solid agreement between the human subjects and the system on the *kind-of* relations. However, these 154 decisions involved only four newspaper articles, so clearly more data would be helpful.

3.3 Automatic Evaluation

While evaluation by humans is valuable, it is expensive to carry out, and this expense must be incurred each time one wants to do an evaluation. Automatic comparison of a machine-generated ontology against reference ontologies constructed by humans, e.g., (Zhang et al. 1996) (Sekine et al. 1999) (Daude et al. 2001), is therefore desirable, provided suitable reference ontologies are available. In this evaluation, the human-generated taxonomy for ProMed described in Section 3.2.1 was used as a reference ontology, with its unlabeled parent-child relation treated as a *kind-of* link. However, the human 'ontology' was created without looking at a corpus, and was developed for use with a different set of goals in mind. Although this involves comparing 'apples' and 'oranges', a comparison is nevertheless illustrative, and can in addition be useful when comparing mutiple ontologies created under similar conditions.

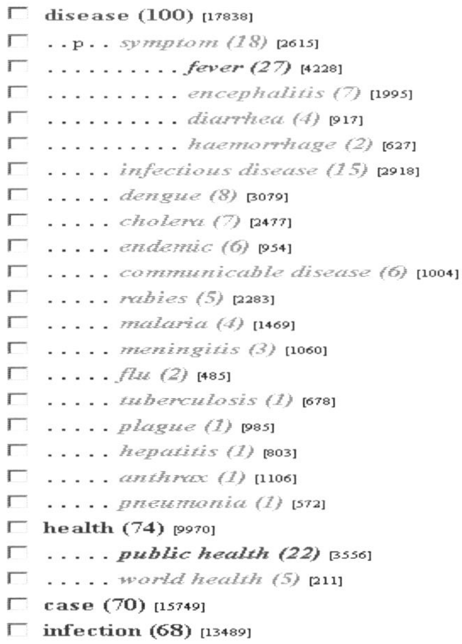

Figure 3: Automatically Induced Fragment from ProMed

To set aside the problem of differences in terminology involved in the comparison, we decided to restrict our attention to the set of terms T_H (of cardinality 3025) in the human ontology (H), and have our system induce relations between them using the ProMed corpus. Relations were induced automatically in the machine ontology (M) for just 761 of those terms, yielding a set T_{H1}. The structure of T_{H1} is shown in a fragment in Figure 3. Here A is a *kind-of* B if it is printed under B without a label; A is a *part-of* B if it is printed under B with a "p" label.

We then automatically computed, for each pair of terms t_1 and t_2 in T_{H1} that were linked distance 1 apart in M, the distance between those terms in H. Likewise, we also computed, for each pair of terms t_1 and t_2 in T_{H1} distance 1 apart in H, the distance between those terms in M.

The results of this comparison are as follows. The number of relations where the two ontologies agree exactly is 63 (i.e., the terms are distance 1 apart in both ontologies). Since, given a set of terms, there are many different ways to construct an ontology, this is encouraging.

The number of relations that our system found which were 'missed', i.e., more than distance 1 away, in H is 1203. Given the previous experiment where the human subjects agreed with the system's relations, these 1203 relations are likely to contain many that the human probably missed. For example, the relations in the machine ontology between 'eye' and 'farsightedness', and 'medicine'

[9] The chi-square for Subphrase Relations is 61.68, and the chi-square for WordNet is 56.73, with $p < 0.001$ in all cases.

and 'chiropractic medicine' are missed by H. This highlights a problem with human-generated ontologies: substantial errors of omission.

The number of relations in H that our system missed (relations that were more than distance 1 away in the system ontology), is 3493. However, of these 3493 relations, 2955 involved at least 1 term that was not included in M, leaving 538 relations that we could calculate the distance for in M. These 538 relations in H include relations between 'acid indigestion medicine' and 'maalox', and 'alternative medicine' and 'acupuncture' (a majority of the misses involved relations between a disease and the name of a specific drug for it, which aren't *part-of* or *kind-of* relations).

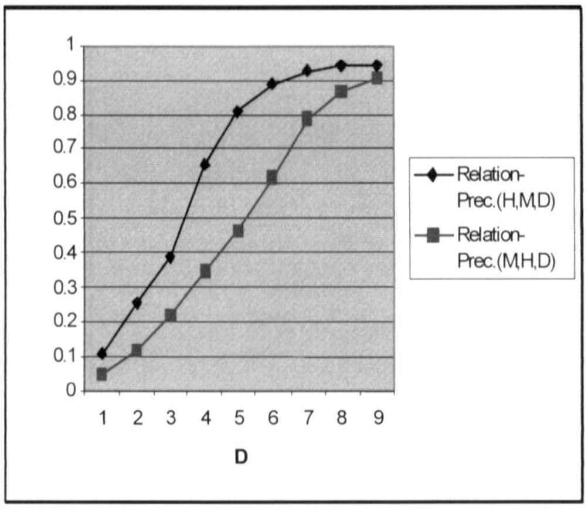

Figure 4: Relation Precision

These observations lead to a metric for comparing one ontology with another one serving as a reference ontology. Given two ontologies A and B, define *Relation Precision (A, B, D)* as t*he proportion of the distance 1 relations in A that are at most a distance D apart in B*. This measure can be plotted for different values of D. In Figure 4, we show the Relation Precision(H, M, D), and Relation Precision(M, H, D), for our machine ontology M and human ontology H. Both curves show Relation Precision(H, M, D) growing faster than Relation Precision(M, H, D), with 70% of the area being below the former curve and 54% being below the latter curve. The graph shows that while 22% of distance 1 relations in M are at most 3 apart in H (but keep in mind the errors of omission in H), 40% of distance 1 relations in H are at most 3 apart in M[10].

[10] The mean distance in H between terms that are distance 1 apart in M is 5.17, with a standard deviation of 2.12. The mean distance in M between terms which are distance 1 apart in H is 3.85, with a standard deviation of 1.69.

4 Related Work

The existing approaches to ontology induction include those that start from structured data, merging ontologies or database schemas (Doan et al. 2002). Other approaches use natural language data, sometimes just by analyzing the corpus (Sanderson and Croft 1999), (Caraballo 1999) or by learning to expand WordNet with clusters of terms from a corpus, e.g., (Girju et al. 2003). Information extraction approaches that infer labeled relations either require substantial hand-created linguistic or domain knowledge, e.g., (Craven and Kumlien 1999) (Hull and Gomez 1993), or require human-annotated training data with relation information for each domain (Craven et al. 1998).

Many, though not all, domain-independent approaches (Evans et al. 1991) (Grefenstette 1997) have restricted themselves to discovering term-associations, rather than labeled relations. A notable exception is (Sanderson and Croft 1995), which (unlike our approach) assumes the existence of a query that was used to originally retrieve the documents (so that terms can be extracted from the query and then expanded to generate additional terms for the ontology). Their approach also is restricted to one method to discover relations, while we use several.

Our approach is complementary to approaches aimed at automatically enhancing existing resources for a particular domain, e.g. (Moldovan et al. 2000). Finally, the prior methods, while they often carry out evaluation, lack standard criteria for ontology evaluation. Although ontology evaluation remains challenging, we have discussed several evaluation methods in this paper.

5 Conclusion

The evidence combination described above is based on transitivity and union. Since the above evaluations, we have been experimenting with an ad hoc weighted evidence combination scheme, based on each knowledge source expressing a strength for a posited relation. In future, we will also investigate using an initial seed ontology to provide a better 'backbone' for induction, and then using a spreading activation method to activate nodes related by existing knowledge sources to seed nodes. Corpus statistics can be used to weight the links. For example, based on (Caraballo 1999), each parent of a leaf node could be viewed as a cluster label for its children, with the weight of a parent-child link being determined based on how strongly the child is associated with the cluster.

The ontology induction methods described here can allow for considerable savings in time in constructing ontologies. The evaluations we have carried out are suggestive, but many issues remain open. There are many unanswered questions about human-created reference ontologies, including lack of inter-annotator agreement studies. Indeed, experience shows that without guidelines for ontology construction, humans are prone to come up with very different ontologies for a domain. Comparing a machine-induced ontology against an ideal human reference ontology, were one to be available, is also fraught with problems. Our experience with using an implementation of the (Daude et al. 2001) constraint relaxation algorithm for ontology comparison suggests that much work is needed on distance metrics which are not over-sensitive to small differences in structure.

Our interest, therefore, is focused more towards an extrinsic evaluation. PRONTO, which is due to be released in 2004, offers the opportunity to measure costs of ontology induction and post-editing on a large-scale problem of value to the biology community. We also plan to measure the effectiveness of PRONTO in query expansion for information access to MEDLINE and protein databases. Finally, we will investigate more sophisticated evidence combination methods, and compare against other automatic methods for ontology induction.

The ontology induction tools are available for free distribution for research purposes.

References

Abney, S. 1996. Partial parsing Via Finite-State Cascades. *Proceedings of the ESSLLI '96 Robust Parsing Workshop*.

Caraballo, S. A. 1999. Automatic Construction of a hypernym-labeled noun hierarchy from text. In *Proceedings of the 37th Annual Meeting of the Association for Computational Linguistics* (ACL'1999), 120-122.

Cohen, P. R., Chaudhri, V., Pease, A. and Schrag, R. 1999. Does Prior Knowledge Facilitate the Development of Knowledge-based Systems? The Sixteenth National Conference on Artificial Intelligence (AAAI-99).

Craven, M. and Kumlien, J. 1999. Constructing biological knowledge bases by extracting information from text sources. *Proc Int Conf Intell Syst Mol Biol.*, 77-86.

Craven, M., DiPasquo, D., Freitag, D., McCallum, A., Mitchell, T., Nigam, K., and Slattery, S.. 1998. Learning to Extract Symbolic Knowledge from the World Wide Web. Proceedings of AAAI-98, 509-516.

Daude, J., Padro, L. and Rigau, G. 2001 A Complete WN1.5 to WN1.6 Mapping. *NAACL-2001 Workshop on WordNet and Other Lexical Resources: Applications, Extension, and Customization*, 83-88.

Doan, A., Madhavan, J. , Domings, P. and Halevy, A. 2002. Learning to Map between Ontologies on the Semantic Web. WWW'2002.

Dunning, T. 1993. Accurate Methods for the Statistics of Surprise and Coincidence," *Computational Linguistics*, 19(1):61-74, 1993.

Girju, R., Badulescu, A., and Moldovan, D. 2003. Learning Semantic Constraints for the Automatic Discovery of Part-Whole Relations. Proceedings of HLT'2003, Edmonton.

Grefenstette, G. 1997. *Explorations in Automatic Thesaurus Discovery.* Kluwer International Series in Engineering and Computer Science, Vol 278.

Hearst, M. 1992. Automatic Acquisition of Hyponyms from Large Text Corpora. *Proceedings of the fourteenth International Conference on Computational Linguistics*, Nantes, France, July 1992.

Hull, R. and Gomez, F. 1993. Inferring Heuristic Classification Hierarchies from Natural Language Input. Telematics and Informatics, 9(3/4), pp. 265-281.

IRS (Internal Revenue Service). 2001. *Tax Guide 2001*. Publication 17. http://www.irs.gov/pub/irs-pdf/p17.pdf

Lawrie, D., Croft, W. B., and Rosenberg, A. 2001. Finding topic words for hierarchical summarization. 24th ACM Intl. Conf. on Research and Development in Information Retrieval, 349-357, 2001.

Miller, G. (1995). WordNet: A Lexical Database for English. *Communications Of the Association For Computing Machinery (CACM)* 38, 39-41.

Sanderson, M. and Croft, B. 1995. Deriving concept hierarchies from text. Proceedings of the 22nd Annual Internationaql ACM SIGIR Conference on Research and Development in Information Retrieval, 160-170.

Sekine, S., Sudo, K. and Ogino, T. 1999. Statistical Matching of Two Ontologies. *Proceedings of ACL SIGLEX99 Workshop: Standardizing Lexical Resources*.

Zhang, K., Wang, J. T. L. and Shasha, D. 1996. On the Editing Distance between Undirected Acyclic Graphs and Related Problems. *International Journal of Foundations of Computer Science* 7, 43-58.

Detecting semantic relations between terms in definitions

Véronique MALAISÉ [1,2] **Pierre ZWEIGENBAUM**[1] **Bruno BACHIMONT** [2]

[1] STIM/AP-HP, ERM 202 INSERM
& CRIM-INaLCO
91, boulevard de l'Hôpital
75013 Paris,
France,
{vma,pz}@biomath.jussieu.fr

[2]DRE de l'INA
Institut National de l'Audiovisuel
4, avenue de l'Europe
94366 Bry-sur-Marne Cedex,
France,
{vmalaise,bbachimont}@ina.fr

Abstract

Terminology structuring aims to elicit semantic relations between the terms of a domain. We propose here to exploit definitions found in corpora to obtain such semantic relations. Definition typologies show that definitions can be introduced by different semantic relations, some of these relations being likely to structure terminologies. Our aim is therefore to mine "defining expressions" in domain-specific corpora, and to detect the semantic relations they involve between their main terms. We use lexico-syntactic markers and patterns to detect at the same time both a definition and its main semantic relation. 46 markers and 74 patterns have been designed and tuned on a first corpus in the field of anthropology. We report on their evaluation on a second corpus in the field of dietetics, where they obtained 4% to 36% recall and from 61 to 66% precision, and discuss the relative accuracy of different subclasses of markers for this task.

1 Introduction

A terminology is an artifact structuring terms according to some semantic relations. Grabar and Hamon (2004) present the different semantic relations likely to be found in terminologies. These can be divided into lexical (synonymy), vertical (hypernymy, meronymy) and transversal relations (domain-specific relations). A study of definition typologies, like the one of (Auger, 1997), shows that these different relations are also present in definitions. We can then hypothesise that mining definitions along with the detection of their inherent semantic relation can help to organise terms according to the relations used in structured terminologies. We focus in this paper on the detection of terms related by hypernymy and synonymy in definitions.

The automatic detection of definitions can rely on different types of existing works. We can, first, consider the studies describing what definition is, and more particularly what definition in corpus is like. In this respect, we can cite the work of Trimble (1985), Flowerdew (1992), Sager (2001) and Meyer (2001). Another type of interesting existing work is about typologies of definitions: Martin (1983), Chukwu and Thoiron (1989) and Auger (1997), amongst others, provide, in their classifications of definitions, linguistic clues to find defining statements in corpus. We propose to integrate the typologies that we mention in section 2.2, along with the linguistic clues they give: the definition markers. And, at last, some works have already focused on mining definitions from corpora, including Cartier (1997), Pearson (1996), Rebeyrolle (2000) and Muresan and Klavans (2002), mostly through the use of lexical definition markers. These works provide us with methodological guidelines and another set of lexical markers for our own experiment.

As (Pearson (1996); Rebeyrolle (2000)), our method is based on lexico-syntactic patterns, so that we can build on the work on French language by Rebeyrolle (2000). We extended her work in two respects: an analysis of the parenthesis as low-level linguistic clue for definitions, and the concomitant extraction of the semantic relation involved in a "defining expression", along with the extraction of the definition itself. Previous works have, for instance, mined definitions to find terms specific to a particular domain of knowledge (Chukwu and Thoiron (1989)), and to describe their meaning (Rebeyrolle, 2000); we focus on the detection of the semantic relations between the main terms of a definition in order to help a terminologist to build a structured terminology following these relations.

We implemented an interface to visualise these definitions and semantic relations extractions. We tuned markers and patterns for extracting definitions and semantic relations on a first corpus about anthropology; we then tested the validity of these markers and patterns on another corpus focused on dietetics. The purpose of this test was, on the one hand, to observe whether definitions were still correctly extracted on the basis of patterns trained on a corpus differing in the domain of knowledge and in the genre of documents involved, and, on the other hand, to detect if the semantic relation associated with each pattern was the same as the one observed in the first corpus. The markers and patterns showed to be comparable to the other experiments mentioned in terms of definition extraction: the precision reached from 61 to 66%. As for the semantic relation associated with the patterns, it obtained different scores, depending on the marker. But, in most cases, one main semantic relation is associated with a pattern in the scope of a single domain, event though a few patterns convey the same relation across our two corpora.

The remainder of this paper is organised as follows: we first present previous work (section 2), describe our method and experiment (section 3), then present and discuss results (section 4) and conclude with directions for future work (section 5).

2 Previous work

2.1 Description of definitions in corpus

As a first approach for detecting and extracting defining statements in corpora, we have to... define this object. In the literature (Trimble (1985); Flowerdew (1992),...), three categories of definitions are often mentioned: the formal definition, the semi-formal and the "non-formal" one. The formal definition follows the Aristotelian schema: X = Y + specific characteristics, where X is the defined term (the *"definiendum"*), "=" means an equivalence relation, Y stands for the generic class to which X belongs (the *"Genus"*), and specific characteristics detail in which respect X is different from the other items composing the same generic class. A semi-formal definition relates the definiendum only with specific characteristics, or with its attribute(s) (Meyer, 2001). Formal and semi-formal definitions can be of simple type (expressed in one sentence), or complex (expressed in two, or more sentences). A non-formal definition aims *"to define in a general sense so that a reader can see the familiar element in whatever the new term may be"* (Trimble, 1985). It can be an association with a synonym, a paraphrase or grammatical derivation.

The common point between all these points of views on the same linguistic object, or between all these different objects sharing the same appellation "definition", is that they all follow the same didactic purpose of disambiguating the meaning of a lexical item, that is to distinguish it from the others in the general language, or inside a specific vocabulary. These definition descriptions present them as the association between a term and its hypernym (its *"genus"*), or between a term and its specific characteristics. But there are yet other ways to express definitions, as the works on their typology shows.

2.2 Typology of definitions

Existing definitions typologies are all dedicated to a specific purpose. We are particularly interested in those which aim at eliciting linguistic clues that can be used to mine defining contexts from corpora. We work on French, for which Martin (1983) has classified dictionary definitions in order to give guidelines for a consistent (electronic) dictionary. In the context of corpus-based research, Chukwu and Thoiron (1989) gave another classification, aiming at finding domain-specific terms in corpora. A unified typology is provided by Auger (1997), compiling both cited typologies along with three others, and from which we draw the following three categories:

- Definitions expressed by "low level" linguistic markers: punctuation clues such as parenthesis, quote, dash, colon;
- Definitions expressed by lexical markers: linguistic or metalinguistic lexical items;
- Definitions expressed by "high level" linguistic markers: syntactic patterns such as anaphora or apposition.

The definitions introduced by lexical means are divided in two branches, characterised by the lexical markers in table 1. We added elements from other studies ((Rebeyrolle, 2000) and (Fuchs, 1994) amongst others), and augmented this typology with

Definitions introduced by linguistic markers	
Copulative	*"a X is a Y that"*
Equivalence	*"equivalent to"*
Characterisation	*"attribute of"*, *"quality"*,...
Analysis	*"composed of"*, *"equipped with"*, *"made of"*,...
Function	*"to have the function"*, *"the role of"*, *"to use X to do Y"*,...
Causality	*"to cause X by Y"*, *"to obtain X by"*,...
Definitions introduced by metalinguistic markers	
Designation	*"to designate"*, *"to mean"*,...
Denomination	*"to name"*
Systemic	*"to write"*, *"to spell"*, *"the noun"*,...

Table 1: Lexical markers (English translation)

new markers, including some items introducing reformulation contexts (*"that is"*, *"to say"*, *"for instance"*, ...).

The Aristotelian definition type is presented here as a "copulative" definition, as it is linguistically marked by the copula "être" (to be). It involves a hypernymic relation (and specific differences) to describe the meaning of a term, so we consider it as a "hypernymic definition". But we can see in table 1 that other semantic relations can also be used to define a term: synonymy (definition of "equivalence" type), meronymy ("analysis" type), causality and other domain-specific transversal relations ("function", "characterisation" types). Mining a definition of "synonymic type" provides different denominations for the same concept; one of "hypernymy type" can help modelling the vertical structure between the *"definiendum"* and the first term of the *"definiens"* (conceptual "father" and "son" association); and definitions following transversal relations allow the expression of specific knowledge. We focus in this paper on the extraction of definitions involving hypernymy and synonymy, which are the most generally considered relations in terminology building.

2.3 Automatic definition mining

Automatic definition mining from corpora can be divided in different groups, according to the methodologies followed. We will illustrate them by describing three recent families of works: (i) Cartier (1997), (ii) Pearson (1996) and Rebeyrolle (2000), (iii) Muresan and Klavans (2002). They have used respectively "contextual exploration", lexico-syntactic patterns and linguistic analysis and rules.

The former one extracts defining statements on the basis of the match of linguistic clues, when they are relayed in the sentence by some linguistic rules. These rules are developped by the author, withing the schema defined in the "contextual exploration" methodology (Desclés, 1996).

Pearson (1996) and Rebeyrolle (2000) have followed the methodology described by Hearst (1992), up to now mainly applied to discover hyponymous terms. It consists in describing the lexico-syntactic context of an occurrence of a pair of terms known to share a semantic relation. Modelling the context in which they occur provides a "pattern" to apply to the corpus, in order to extract other pairs of terms connected by the same relation. Pearson and Rebeyrolle have modelled lexico-syntactic contexts around lexical clues interpreted as "definition markers". Rebeyrolle, working on French, evaluated the different pattern types she modelled, across different corpora: she obtained a precision range of 17.95 – 79.19%, and a recall of 94.75 – 100%. The difference between the two numeric boundaries of the precision range is due to the kind of markers involved in the lexico-syntactic pattern evaluated: metalinguistic markers obtained a high precision rate, but not linguistic lexical markers.

The latter pair of authors have based their system DEFINDER (`http://www1.cs.columbia.edu/~smara/DEFINDER/`) on the lexical and syntactic analysis of a medical corpus, with semi-automatic definition acquisition. Their evaluation is focused on the usefulness of the system, as compared with existing specialised medical dictionaries. They reach a 86.95% precision and 75.47% recall, following their evaluation methodology.

We chose to follow the first methodology in our experiment (see section 3), in which we additionally explore definition mining in some cases where the definition is not introduced by lexical items. Following this methodology enables us to build on existing work dedicated to French, which showed to be interesting and efficient. The lexico-syntactic pattern methodology also enables us to access the different linguistic elements we were interested in mining: the definition itself, the main terms of the definition and the semantic relation between them. We focus this experimentation more particularly on identifying the semantic relations of synonymy and hypernymy involved in the different definitions likely to be found in corpora. We aim at testing whether a stable link can be established between the definition extraction pattern and a specific semantic relation.

3 Detecting Semantic Relations

Our goal is to automatically detect some of the semantic relations that might be found in definitions and to propose them to a human validator in charge of structuring a terminology. We focus on hypernymy and synonymy, which are the most classical relations found in terminology. If the relation is hypernymy, the terms are to be modelled in a hierarchical way, if it is synonymy, both terms can be used to express the same concept. The relations and the definitions are extracted together from corpora, by the same lexico-syntactic patterns. We present in the next subsections our two corpora (section 3.1), then the lexico-syntactic patterns we used (section 3.2) and their experimental evaluation (section 3.3): we analyse whether a relation found in connection with a lexico-syntactic pattern in the training corpus can be unchanged in the context of the same lexico-syntactic pattern, when applied to a different corpus.

3.1 Description and preparation of the corpora

Our training corpus (76 Kwords) is focused on childhood, from the point of view of anthropologists. It is composed of different genres of documents (documentary descriptions, thesis report extracts, Web documents). Documentary descriptions were humanly collected, whereas electronic documents were automatically collected from Internet via the tools of (Grabar and Berland, 2001). Our evaluation corpus (480 Kwords), in the domain of dietetics, is composed of Web documents indexed by the CISMeF quality-controlled catalog of French medical Web sites (`http://www.chu-rouen.fr/cismef/`) in the subtrees "Dietetics" and "Nutrition" of the MeSH thesaurus. It is mainly composed of medical courses and Web pages presenting information about nutrition in different medical contexts. Both corpora were morpho-syntactically analysed by Cordial Analyser (Synapse Developpement, `http://www.synapse-fr.com/`). Cordial tags, lemmatises and parses a corpus, yielding grammatical functions (subject, object, ...) between chunks.

3.2 Lexico-syntactic patterns

A given linguistic marker (see, *e.g.*, table 1) can occur in different contexts, some of which are definitions, and can be a clue for different semantic relations. Lexico-syntactic patterns aim at reducing this ambiguity by specifying more restricted contexts in which a definition is found, and, furthermore, in which one specific semantic relation is involved.

Unlike (Hearst, 1992), we started the pattern design by analysing marker occurrences in our training corpus. We designed and tuned our lexico-syntactic patterns on this corpus, patterns dedicated to the extraction of definitions and specific relations: hypernymy and synonymy. Our patterns use the information output by the parser, including lemma, morpho-syntactic category and grammatical function. For instance: *"N (N)"* specifies that the marker *"("* has to be preceded by a noun, and immediately followed by a single common noun, followed by a closing parenthesis. In this specific case, *"("* introduces a hypernymic definition.

Each pattern drives different kinds of processing:

- extraction of the defining sentence on the basis of the whole pattern;
- selection of one "preferred" relation associated with the specific pattern, among the set of possible relations associated with the marker; this relation stands between the interdefined terms of the definition;
- extraction of the interdefined terms following two strategies (contextual or based on dependencies around the marker), depending on the morphosyntactic category of the marker. When the marker is a punctuation or a noun, we usually extract its left and right syntactic contexts[1] (roughly the first chunk before the marker, and the first chunk after the marker in the sentence). When the marker is a verb, we extract its subject and object if they exist in the sentence, otherwise we extract its left and right chunks, as in the previous case.

Our patterns are implemented in XSLT and the resulting extractions are shown to a human validator through a Web interface (figure 1): an HTML form allowing the validator to complete and correct the extractions. It is possible for the validator to correct the terms extracted from the definition, in particular because the chunk often includes punctuation, which is usually not considered as part of the term, and it is possible to select a different semantic relation than the one proposed when it happens not to be the correct one. A combo box shows all the possible relations related to the marker involved in the lexico-syntactic pattern which provided the extraction of the defining sentence.

3.3 Experimental setup

We tuned our lexico-syntactic patterns to extract definitions from the test corpus. We associated with each pattern a "preferential" semantic relation, which human corpus analysis showed to be the more likely to be connected to the definitions extracted by the means of this pattern. The aim of the experiment is to test the stability of this connection, by applying the patterns to the evaluation corpus.

A random sample of the test corpus (13 texts among 132) was manually processed to tag its definitions, in order to have a standard measure for the evaluation of recall. Table 2 shows the number of definitions of synonymic and hypernymic types found in that sample, and provides the percentages of these definitions among all the different kinds of tagged definitions (*"% definitions"*) in that sample. Some definitions involved more than one semantic relation, so we also present the percentage of hypernymic and synonymic relations among all the semantic relations (*"% relations"*).

[1]Depending on the position of the marker in the sentence, it might be the two following or two preceding chunks.

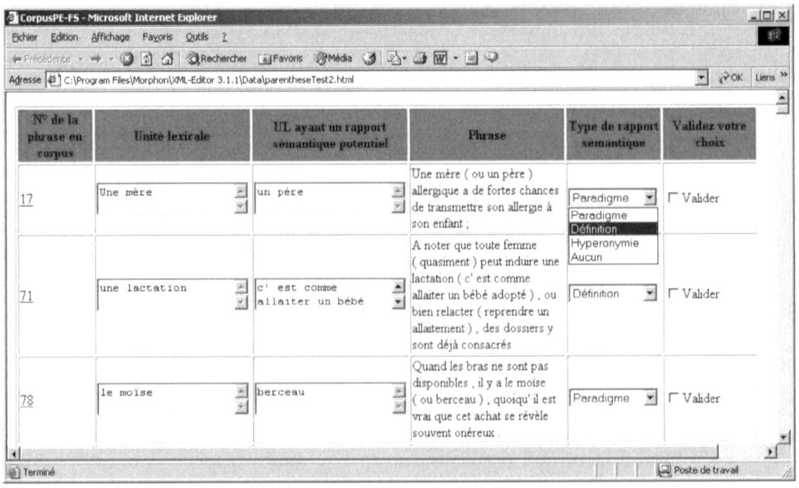

Figure 1: Human validation interface for definitions extracted with the parenthesis marker

	Hypernymy	Synonymy
# definitions	90	22
% definitions	44, 5%	10, 8%
% relations	39, 1%	9, 5%

Table 2: Number and percentages of hypernymic and synonymic definitions in a random sample of the test corpus, according to the human evaluator

In our experiment, we evaluate in turn the quality of the extracted definitions, then that of semantic relations (hypernymy and synonymy).

4 Results and discussion

Table 3 shows the number of markers and patterns prepared and tuned on the training corpus to extract definitions based on hypernymy or synonymy. Note that a given marker can be used in different patterns to extract different semantic relations. Some markers were also associated in one pattern: the metalinguistic nouns and verbs. We combined them because their individual recall was not lowered by this association and their precision score was improved. The sentences below are examples of sentences extracted by our system; the underlined part is the marker:

	Hypernymy	Synonymy
# markers	3	43
# patterns	4	70

Table 3: Number of markers and patterns

- Hypernymic relation:
  "Les acides gras de la série omega-3 (MAX-epa) peuvent également être prescrits .",
  "[...]*les fromages à pâte cuite (tels que par exemple le fromage de Hollande).*"
- Synonymic relation:
  "L' activité physique est définie comme tout mouvement corporel produit par la contraction des muscles squelettiques ,[...]",
  "une relation inverse entre l' activité physique et l' insulinémie ou la sensibilité à l' insuline est habituellement observée ."

Table 4 presents the evaluation results: we divide them according to the semantic relation extracted. It shows the number of definitions retrieved, and the associated precision and recall. Precision is divided in two measures.

	Hypernymy	Synonymy
# extracted sentences	270	585
Precision (def)	61%	66%
Precision (rel)	26%	15%
Recall (rel)	4%	36%

Table 4: Evaluation of precision (test corpus) and recall (random sample of test corpus)

- the proportion of extracted sentences that corresponded to definitions (*def*), and
- the proportion of correct semantic relations found in retrieved definitions (*rel*).

Recall is the proportion of retrieved definitions which correctly display the semantic relation *identified in the sample corpus* among all the definitions present in this sample which were tagged as having this semantic relation by the human evaluator.[2]

The precision of extracted definitions is comparable to Rebeyrolle's results. The precision of semantic relations is much lower, but a global evaluation does not show the particular behavior of some of the markers. We list below the markers which were actually involved in the extraction of definitions in the test corpus.

- Markers implied in hypernymic definition retrieval: *"parenthèse"* (parenthesis), *"par exemple"* (for instance), *"sorte de"* (a kind of);
- Markers implied in synonymic definition retrieval: *"parenthèse"* (parenthesis), *"il s'agit de"* (as for), *"indiquer"* (to indicate), *"soit"* (that is), *"expliquer"* (to explain), *"préciser"* (to specify), *"marquer"* (to mark), *"enfin"* (say), *"ou"* (or), *"comme"* (as), *"à savoir"* (that is), *"autrement dit"* (in other words), *"au sens de"* (meaning), *"équivaloir"* (to be equivalent), *"c'est-à-dire"* (that is), *"définir"* (to define), *"désigner"* (to designate), *"nommer"* (to name), *"dénommer"* (to name), *"référer"* (to refer), *"expression"* (expression), *"terme"* (term).

Table 5 presents the different semantic relations found in the definitions retrieved by each marker. The first column references the markers involved in the extraction of the definition, the second (*"Expected"*) presents the number of definitions, extracted by each marker, following the expected relation. *"Other"* gives the number of retrieved definitions following another semantic relation, *"Undecidable"* represents the number of definitions for which we could not determine the semantic relation,[3] and *"Non definition"* presents the number of retrieved sentences that were not definitions.[4]

Definitions retrieved with the hypernymy patterns involved very generic markers, and they introduced a number of other semantic relations. The pattern around *"for instance"*, for which 16 extracted sentences out of 95 were not definitions, can still be specified to discriminate defining contexts from others. We can notice, though, that it is one of the most productive patterns (95 extractions) and that it reaches a $47,3\%$ precision. But the patterns around the parenthesis show that the same syntactic context can introduce different kinds of relations: in this case, the lexico-syntactic pattern cannot disambiguate the relation any further. The pattern *"N (N)"* introduced "hypernymic definitions", as well as "synonymic" or "meronymic" ones, the same syntactic context being even likely to be interpreted as a transversal relation between a treatment and a disease, for instance. It is the sentence as a whole that has to be interpreted in order to be able to define the relevant semantic relation between the terms in that syntactic context.

Some linguistic markers (as *"comme"*) are reliable for detecting a semantic relation: 9 sentences out of 13 were "synonymic definitions". But surprisingly enough, some metalinguistic verbs (*"définir"*, for instance) were not as effective as them in that purpose. *"Définir"* introduced only 22 "synonymic definitions" out of 68 sentences retrieved. One could think that a verb with metalinguistic function could be less polysemic than another of more "generic purpose". This naive hope happens to be wrong: *"Définir"* means "to fix (a limit)" as often as "to define". Some markers steadily introduced a semantic relation, but not the one they were supposed to: this variation is probably due to the change in domains across our two corpora. And some patterns obviously introduced a definition, but the defined element was in the previous sentence (this is the case of 92 extractions with patterns involving the marker *"Il s'agit de"*). As our system, up to now, extracts only one sentence, we could not determine whether the semantic relation was the one expected. We must address this problem, and we can hope that the precision rate will then be better than the one presented here: some sentences for which we could not interpret the semantic relation might convey the one we expected. The best precision score is reached by patterns involving two markers: a metalinguistic noun associated with a metalinguistic verb. In a more general way, analysing the defining sentences extracted, we could see that sentences that were the "best" definitions (the closest to dictionary definitions) often

[2]The percentage of definitions of hypernymic and synonymic type among all definitions in the sample of the test corpus is given in table 2.

[3]Because our system extracts only one sentence, and a larger context was necessary to understand the semantic relation involved, or because of a problem in the conversion of some HTML documents to texts for the evaluation corpus.

[4]Except sentences presenting terms in a paradigm context, which is also interesting for terminology structuring. We included this paradigm context in the *"Other"* column.

Marker	Expected	Other	Undecidable	Non definition	Total
Parenthesis (Parenthèse)	Hyp: 25	Meronymy: 1, Synonymy: 38 (+3), Transversal: 7	4	84	163
For instance (Par exemple)	Hyp: 45	Transversal: 2	32	16	95
A kind of (Une sorte de)	Hyp: 1	Transversal: 2	5	5	13
Parenthesis (Parenthèse)	Syn: 10	Paradigm: 9	2	4	25
As for (Il s'agit de)	Syn: 10	Transversal: 4, Hypernymy: 1	**92**	9	115
To indicate (Indiquer)	Syn: 5	Transversal: 12	6	**77**	100
That is (Soit)	Syn: 7	Paradigm: 31, Transversal: 13	15	1	66
To explain (Expliquer)	Syn: 1	Transversal: 21	15	**28**	65
To specify (Spécifier)	Syn:1	Transversal: 5	9	**26**	41
To mark (Marquer)	Syn: 1	Transversal: 7	6	12	26
Say (Enfin)	Syn: 0	Paradigm: 3	2	1	6
Or (Ou)	Syn: 3	Paradigm: 23	1	0	27
As (Comme)	Syn: 9	Paradigm: 1	1	2	13
That is (A savoir)	Syn: 4	Hypernymy: 3	5	0	12
In other words (Autrement dit)	Syn: 1	0	2	0	3
Equivalent to (équivaloir)	Syn: 0	0	4	0	4
To define (Définir)	Syn: 22	Transversal: 8	19	19	68
To designate (Désigner)	Syn: 3	Hypernymy: 0	0	0	3
Term (Terme)	Syn: 1	0	1	0	2
Meaning (Au sens de)	Syn: 0	0	1	0	1
That is (C'est-à-dire)	Syn: 1	0	0	0	1
To name (Nommer)	Syn: 0	0	2	1	3
To name (Dénommer)	Syn: 1	0	0	0	1
To refer to (Référer)	Syn: 0	0	0	2	2
Expression (Expression)	Syn: 0	1	1	0	2

Table 5: Semantic relations in retrieved definitions

involved two or even three markers. This underlines the interest of introducing a relevance measure that takes into account the number of markers present in the sentence.

5 Conclusions

Our experiment tried to link the semantic relation inherent to different kinds of definitions with the marker (the heart of our lexico-syntactic patterns) and more specifically with the lexico-syntactic patterns at the origin of the extraction of the definition itself. Having a close look at some of the markers, we can observe that some linguistic items can be very reliable markers for definition extraction associated with a semantic relation. We can also find out that the polysemy of some markers is related to the domain of the corpus. In that respect, the reusability of the lexico-syntactic patterns is limited to a set of markers which were found to be reliable across our two corpora. What is more problematic is the fact that it is sometimes not possible to make a specific distinction between different semantic relations detected with the same marker in the context of definitions sharing most of their syntactic contexts. But most of the patterns retrieve a good rate of defining sentences, some patterns being more reliable than others; and the more numerous the markers involved, the more likely it is that we have a definition. And usually these patterns retrieve definitions following one main semantic relation (this is not the case however for parenthesis and the patterns involving the marker *"à savoir"*). This leads to the hypothesis that if lexico-syntactic patterns may not be used to propose semantic relations that are valid across different domains, they remain a good clue for mining definitions, especially definitions of one type of semantic relation *inside* a given domain. Moreover, given a new corpus, applying the existing patterns to a sub-corpus could lead to the elicitation of the associated semantic relations for that corpus, which could be a relevant methodology to discover pairs of terms following these associated relations.

References

A. Auger. 1997. *Repérage des énoncés d'intérêt définitoire dans les bases de données textuelles.* Thèse de doctorat, Université de Neuchâtel.

E. Cartier. 1997. La définition dans les textes scientifiques et techniques : présentation d'un outil d'extraction automatique de relations définitoires. *2e Rencontres "Terminologie et Intelligence Artificielle" (TIA'97)*, Equipe de Recherche en Syntaxe et Sémantique. Toulouse, 3-4 avril 1997:127–140.

U. Chukwu and P. Thoiron. 1989. Reformulation et repérage des termes. *La Banque des Mots*, Numéro spécial CTN - INaLF - CNRS:23–53.

J.-P. Desclés. 1996. Systèmes d'exploration contextuelle. *Table ronde sur le Contexte*, avril 1996, Caen.

J. Flowerdew. 1992. Definitions in science lectures. *Linguistics*, vol.13 (2):202–221.

C. Fuchs. 1994. *Paraphrase et énonciation.* Paris, Ophrys.

N. Grabar and S. Berland. 2001. Construire un corpus web pour l'acquisition terminologique. *4e rencontres Terminologie et Intelligence Artificielle (TIA 2001)*, Nancy:44–54.

N. Grabar and T. Hamon. 2004. Les relations dans les terminologies structurées : de la théorie à la pratique. *Revue d'Intelligence Artificielle (RIA)*, 18-1:57–85.

M. Hearst. 1992. Automatic acquisition of hyponyms from large text corpora. *15th International Conference on Computational Linguistics (COLING 1992)*, Nantes:539–545.

R. Martin. 1983. *Pour une logique du sens.* Paris, PUF.

I. Meyer. 2001. Extracting knowledge-rich contexts for terminography. In D. Bourigault, editor, *Recent advances in Computational Terminology*, pages 279–302. John Benjamins Publishing Company, Philadelphia, PA.

S. Muresan and J. L. Klavans. 2002. A method for automatically building and evaluating dictionary resources. *the language Resources and Evaluation Conference (LREC 2002)*, Las Palmas, Spain:231–234.

J. Pearson. 1996. The expression of definitions in specialised texts: a corpus-based analysis. In M. Gellerstam, J. Järborg, S. G. Malmgren, K. Norén, L.Rogström, and C. Papmehl, editors, *7th International Congress on Lexicography (EURALEX'96)*, pages 817–824. Göteborg University, Göteborg, Sweden.

J. Rebeyrolle. 2000. *Forme et fonction de la définition en discours.* Thèse de doctorat, Université de Toulouse II - Le Mirail.

J. C. Sager. 2001. *Essays on Definition.* John Benjamins, Amsterdam.

L. Trimble. 1985. *English for Science and Technology: A Discourse Approach.* Cambridge University Press, Cambridge.

Discovering Synonyms and Other Related Words

Krister LINDÉN and Jussi PIITULAINEN
Helsinki University, Department of General Linguistics,
P.O.Box 9 (Siltavuorenpenger 20 A),
FIN-00014 University of Helsinki,
Finland,
Krister.Linden@helsinki.fi, Jussi.Piitulainen@helsinki.fi

Abstract

Discovering synonyms and other related words among the words in a document collection can be seen as a clustering problem, where we expect the words in a cluster to be closely related to one another. The intuition is that words occurring in similar contexts tend to convey similar meaning.

We introduce a way to use translation dictionaries for several languages to evaluate the rate of synonymy found in the word clusters. We also apply the information radius to calculating similarities between words using a full dependency syntactic feature space, and introduce a method for similarity recalculation during clustering as a fast approximation of the high-dimensional feature space. Finally, we show that 69-79 % of the words in the clusters we discover are useful for thesaurus construction.

1 Introduction

Finding related words among the words in a document collection can be seen as a clustering problem, where we expect the words in a cluster to be closely related to the same sense or to be distributional substitutes or proxies for one another. A number of language-technology tasks can benefit from such word clusters, e.g. document classification applications, language modelling, resolving prepositional phrase attachment, conjunction scope identification, word sense disambiguation, word sense separation, automatic thesaurus generation, information retrieval, anaphor resolution, text simplification, topic identification, spelling correction (Weeds, 2003).

At present, synonyms and other related words are available in manually constructed ontologies, such as synonym dictionaries, thesauri, translation dictionaries and terminologies. Manually constructing ontologies is time-consuming even for a single domain. On the world-wide web there are documents on many topics in different languages that could benefit from having an ontology. For many of them some degree of automation is eventually needed.

Humans often infer the meaning of an unknown word from its context. Lets look at a less well-known word like *blopping*. We look it up on the Web. Some of the hits are: *Blopping through some of my faves*, i.e. leafing through favourite web links, *A blop module emits strange electronic blopping noises*, i.e. an electronic sound, *The volcano looked like something off the cover of a Tolkien novel - perfectly conical, billowing smoke and blopping out chunks of bright orange lava*, i.e. spluttering liquid. At first we find all of them different and perhaps equally important. When looking at further links, we get an intuition that the first instance is perhaps a spurious creative metonym, whereas the two others can be regarded as more or less conventional and represent two distinct senses of *blopping*. However, the meaning of all three seems to be related to a sound, which is either clicking or spluttering in nature.

The intuition is that words occurring in the same or similar contexts tend to convey similar meaning. This is known as the Distributional Hypothesis (Harris, 1968). There are many approaches to computing semantic similarity between words based on their distribution in a corpus. For a general overview of similarity measures, see (Manning and Schütze, 1999), and for some recent and extensive overviews and evaluations of similarity measures for i.a. automatic thesaurus construction, see (Weeds, 2003; Curran, 2003; Lee, 2001; Dagan et al., 1999). They show that the information radius and the α-skew distance are among the best for finding distributional proxies for words.

If we assume that a word w is represented as a sum of its contexts and that we can calculate the similarities between such word representations, we get a list L_w of words with quantifications of how similar they are to w. Each similarity list L_w contains a mix of words related to the senses of the word w.

If we wish to identify groups of synonyms and other related words in a list of similarity-rated words, we need to find clusters of similar words that are more similar to one another than they are to other words. For a review of general clustering algorithms, see (Jain et al., 1999) and for a recent evaluation of clustering algorithms for finding word categories, see (Pantel, 2003). (Pantel, 2003) shows that among the standard algorithms the average-link and the k-means clustering perform the best when trying to discover meaningful word groups.

In order to evaluate the quality of the discovered clusters three methods can be used, i.e. measuring the internal coherence of clusters, embedding the clusters in an application, or evaluating against a manually generated answer key. The first method is generally used by the clustering algorithms themselves. The second method is especially relevant for applications that can deal with noisy clusters and avoids the need to generate answer keys specific to the word clustering task. The third method requires a gold standard such as WordNet or some other ontological resource. For an overview of evaluation methodologies for word clustering, see (Weeds, 2003; Curran, 2003; Pantel, 2003).

The contribution of this article is four-fold. The first contribution is to *apply the information radius in a full dependency syntactic feature space* when calculating the similarities between words. Previously, only a restricted set of dependency relations has been applied. The second contribution is a *similarity recalculation during clustering*, which we introduce as a fast approximation of high-dimensional feature space and study its effect on some standard clustering algorithms. The third contribution is a simple but efficient way to *evaluate the synonym content of clusters by using translation dictionaries for several languages*. Finally we show that *69-79 % of the words in the discovered clusters are useful* for thesaurus construction.

The rest of this article is organized as follows. Section 2 presents the corpus data and the the feature extraction. Section 3 introduces the discovery methodology. Section 4 presents the evaluation methodology. In Section 5 we present the experiments and evaluate the results and their significance. Sections 6 and 7 contain the discussion and conclusion, respectively.

2 Corpus Data

Our corpus consists of nouns in a sentence context. We used all the nouns (in base form) that occurred more than 100 times (in any inflected form) in a corpus of Finnish newspaper text. The corpus contained 245 000 documents totaling 48 million words of the Finnish newspaper *Helsingin sanomat* from 1995–1997. Excluding TV and radio listings, there were 196 000 documents with 42 million words. As corpus data we selected all the 17 835 nouns occurring more than 100 times comprising 14 million words of the corpus.

3 Methodology

First we present the types of features we have extracted from the corpus. Then we briefly describe the similarity measure which we use in order to calculate the similarity between the nouns in the corpus data. We also introduce a method for creating derived similarity information in a low-dimensional space. Finally we present the clustering algorithms which we apply to the similarity information.

3.1 Feature extraction

The present experiments aim at discovering the nouns that are most similar in meaning to a given noun. The assumption is that words occurring in similar syntactic contexts belong to the same semantic categories (Harris, 1968). In order to determine the similarity of the syntactic contexts, we represent a word w as a probability distribution over a set of features a occurring in the context of w: $P(a|w)$. The context features a are the major class words w' (nouns, adjectives and verbs) with direct dependency links to the word w. The context feature is the word w' in base form labeled with the dependency relation r. For example, the noun might occur as an object of a verb and with an adjective modifier; both the verb and the adjective including their dependency relations are context features.

We used Connexor's dependency parser FDG for Finnish (Connexor, 2002) for parsing the corpus. A sample of the parser output is shown in Table 1. Tokens of each sentence are numbered starting from zero, each token is on its own line, the token number first, the actual word form second and the base form in the third field. The fourth field links dependent tokens to their heads using a grammatical label and the

#	Token	Base form	Dependency	Morphosyntax	Gloss
0					
1	Toisessa	toinen		&NH PRON SG INE	In the other
2	esitetään	esittää	main:>0	&+MV V PASS IND PRES	they showed
3	videoita	video	obj:>2	&NH N PL PTV	videos
4	ja	ja	cc:>3	&CC CC	and
5	filmejä	filmi	cc:>3	&NH N PL PTV	films
6	.	.			
7	<s>	<s>	>6		

Table 1: Sample output from the FDG parser for Finnish (with an English gloss added).

number of the head token. The fifth field contains morphosyntactic information.

Two tokens, 3 and 5, are labeled as nouns `N`. The noun `video` is a direct object to the verb `esittää`, and the noun `filmi` is coordinated with `video`, so `video` gets two feature occurrences from this sentence:

```
esittää-obj
cc-filmi.
```

Also, `filmi` gets

```
video-cc
```

as a feature occurrence. The pronoun `toinen` is not a potential feature because of its word class and because it is not linked. The coordinating conjunction `ja` is not a potential feature because of its word class.

The parsed corpus contained a total of 18 516 609 unambiguous noun occurrences, 69 314 noun/verb ambiguities, 39 104 noun/adjective ambiguities, 20 847 noun/adverb ambiguities and 11 739 noun/numeral ambiguities, i.e. the amount of remaining ambiguities was less than 0.8 %. When its analyses were underspecified with more than one morphological analysis remaining, we took the relatively small risk ($p < 0.008$) of committing to a noun analysis.

As a straightforward weighting of the context features of a word, we used the number of occurrences with all the instances of the word. In our choice of similarity formula, the representation of a word w must be a probability distribution. This is formally just a matter of normalizing the weights of the features. Thus, a word w is represented as $w : a \mapsto P(a|w)$, i.e. the conditional probability distribution of all features a given the word w, such that $\sum_a P(a|w) = 1$.

Extracting features only from direct dependency relations produces few feature occurrences for each instance of a noun. This keeps the number of distinct features tolerable for all but the most frequent words, and still retains the most promising co-occurring words. As we use only linear frequency weighting, very frequent features tend to get more weight than they should. Additionally, many rare features could have been dropped without much loss of information.

3.2 Similarity calculations

In (Weeds, 2003; Lee, 2001), i.a. the information radius is applied to finding words that can be used as proxies or substitutes for one another. Their tests show that the information radius is among the best for finding such words. Here we briefly recapitulate the details of the similarity estimate, which is rather an estimate of dissimilarity.

Two words are distributionally similar to the extent that they co-occur with the same words, i.e., to the extent that they share features. We define the dissimilarity of two words, p and q, as

$$J(p,q) = (D(p\|m) + D(q\|m))/2, \qquad (1)$$

where $D(p\|m) = \sum_a p(a)(\log_2 p(a) - \log_2 m(a))$ and $m(a) = (p(a) + q(a))/2$ for any feature a. This is the symmetrically weighted case of the Jensen–Shannon divergence (Lin, 1991), also known as the information radius or the mean divergence to the mean (Dagan et al., 1999). For complete identity, $J(p,p) = 0$. For completely disjoint feature sets, $J(p,q) = 1$. The formula is symmetric but does not satisfy the triangle inequality. For speed the estimate may be calculated from the shared features alone (Lee, 1999).

After calculating all the pairwise estimates, we retained lists of the 100 most similar nouns for each of the nouns in the corpus data. No other data is used in the similarity calculations.

3.3 Low-dimensional similarity measures

Performing all the calculations in high-dimensional feature space is time-consuming. Here we introduce a method that can be used as an approximation in low-dimensional feature space based on the initial similarity estimates.

Assume that we have lists of the words that are distributionally most similar to a given word w. Each list L_w contains 100 words with an estimate of their similarity to w. The words in L_w represent a mix of the different meanings of the word w. We create a similarity matrix dis_w for these words such that $dis_w(p,q) = J(p,q)$, where $p, q \in L_w$. The similarity matrix dis_w is a symmetric matrix of the dimensions 101 by 101, as we also include the word w in the matrix.

A vector $p_w = dis_w(p,.)$ in the similarity matrix dis_w is regarded as a projection of the word p from a high dimensional feature space onto a 101-dimensional space, i.e. p is projected onto the 101 most important dimensions of w. The new matrix is not orthogonal, so we apply single-value decomposition (SVD) $dis_w = T\,S\,D$ and use T to rotate the matrix so that the first axis runs along the direction of the largest variation among the word similarity estimates, the second dimension runs along the direction of the second largest variation and so forth. After this rotation we can cluster the new vectors $p_{w,T} = T^t\, p_w$ as low-dimensional representatives of the original high-dimensional feature space. Often SVD is used for dimensionality reduction, but here we use its left singular vectors only for rotating the matrix in order to achieve noise reduction during clustering.

In the new low-dimensional vector representation $p_{w,T}$ we apply the cosine distance $cosd(p_{w,T}, q_{w,T}) = 1 - \cos(p_{w,T}, q_{w,T})$ in order to calculate the similarity between words. As a comparison we also tried the squared Euclidean distance $eucld(p_{w,T}, q_{w,T}) = \|p_{w,T} - q_{w,T}\|^2$ between words in the low-dimensional space. We first normalize the vectors to unit length, which effectively makes the squared Euclidean distance the same as two times the cosine distance: $\|A-B\|^2 = \|A\|^2 + \|B\|^2 - 2\|A\|\,\|B\|\,\cos(A,B)$, and when $\|A\| = 1$ and $\|B\| = 1$, we have $\|A-B\|^2 = 2\,(1 - \cos(A,B))$.

3.4 Clustering

When we wish to discover the potential senses of w by clustering, we are currently only interested in the 100 words in L_w with a similarity estimate for w. The other words are deemed to be too dissimilar to w to be relevant.

We cluster the words related to w with standard algorithms such as complete-link and average-link clustering (Manning and Schütze, 1999). Complete-link and average-link are hierarchical clustering methods. We compare them with flat clustering methods like k-means and self-organizing maps (SOM) (Kohonen, 1997). In k-means the clusters have no ordering. The potential benefit of using SOM with a two-dimensional display compared to k-means is that related data samples get assigned into nearby clusters as the SOM converges forming cluster areas with related content.

We use the MATLAB implementation (The MathWorks, Inc., 2002) of the algorithms. We use both the original similarity measures in dis_w and the distance measures $cosd$ and $eucld$, which we defined on the low-dimensional space. In order to use methods like k-means and SOM, we need to be able to calculate the similarity between cluster centroids and words to be clustered each time a centroid is updated. We do this in the low-dimensional space $p_{w,T}$ using $cosd$ and $eucld$.

For SOM, the MATLAB implementation supported only the squared Euclidean distance. It should be noted that the centroids are not necessarily of unit length, so the squared Euclidean distance is different from the cosine distance between the samples and the centroids, when the centroids are based on more than one sample.

Our clustering setup currently produces hard clusters, where each word w in L_w belong to one cluster, as opposed to soft clustering, where a word may belong to several clusters. We call the cluster containing the word w itself the key cluster.

4 Evaluation methodology

In order to evaluate the quality of the clusters we need a gold standard. English and a number of other languages have resources such as WordNet (Fellbaum, 1998; Vossen, 2001). For Finnish there is no WordNet and there are no large on-line synonym dictionaries available. In fact, our experiment can be seen as a feasibility study for automatically extracting information that could be used for building a WordNet for Finnish. The synsets of WordNet contain synonyms, so we can evaluate the feasibility of the clusters for WordNet development by rating the amount of synonyms and related words in the

Language	Target word	Back translation
English	deficit	*vaje, vajaus, alijäämä*; *tilivajaus*
	shortfall	*vaje, alijäämä*
German	Defizit	*vajaus, vaje, alijäämä*; kassavajaus, tappio; *tilivajaus*; puutos, puute
	Unterbilanz	*alijäämä, vajaus, vaje*, kauppavaje
	Fehlbetrag	*vajaus, alijäämä*, tappio, virhemaksu
French	déficit	*alijäämä*, miinus, *tilivajaus*; *vajaus, vaje*; tappio

Table 2: Translations of the Finnish source word *alijäämä* into English, German and French with the back translations into Finnish. The shared back translations *vaje, vajaus, alijäämä, tilivajaus* are highlighted.

discovered clusters.

We note that when translating a word from the source language the meaning of the word is rendered in a target language. Such meaning preserving relations are available in translation dictionaries. If we translate into the target language and back we end up i.a. with the synonyms of the original source language word. In addition, we may also get some spurious words that are related to other meanings of the target language words. If we assume that the other words represent spurious cases of polysemy or homonymy in the target language, we can reduce the impact of these spurious words by considering several target languages and for each source word we use only the back-translated source words that are common to all the target languages. We call such a group of words a source word synonym set. For an example, see Table 2.

In addition to the mechanical rating of the synonym content we also manually classified the words of some cluster samples into synonymy, antonymy, hyperonymy, hyponymy, complementarity and other relations.

4.1 Evaluation data

In order to evaluate the clusters we picked a random sample of 1759 nouns from the corpus data, which represented approximately 10 % of the words we had clustered. For these words we extracted the translations in the Finnish-English, Finnish-German and Finnish-French MOT dictionaries (Kielikone, 2004) available in electronic form. We then translated each target language word back into Finnish using the same resources. The dictionaries are based on extensive hand-made dictionaries. The choice of words may be slightly different in each of them, which means that the words in common for all the dictionaries after the back translation tend to be only the core synonyms.

For evaluation purposes it would be unfair to demand that the clustering generate words into the clusters that are not in the corpus data, so we also removed those back translations from the source word synonym sets. Finally, only synonym sets that had more than one word remaining were interesting, i.e. they contained more than the original source word. There were 453 of the 1759 test words that met the qualifications. The average number of synonyms or back translations for these test words was 3.53 including the source word itself.

For manual classification we used a sample of 50 key clusters from the whole set of clusters and an additional sample of 50 key clusters from the words qualifying for the mechanical evaluation.

4.2 Evaluation method

The mechanical evaluation was performed by picking the key cluster produced by a clustering algorithm for each of the test words. The key cluster was the cluster which contained the original source word. The evaluation was a simple overlap calculation with the gold standard generated from the translation dictionaries. By counting the number of cluster words in a source word synonym set and dividing by the synonym set size, we get the recall R. By counting the number of of source word synonyms in a cluster and dividing by the cluster size, we get the precision P.

The manual evaluation was performed independently by the two authors and an external linguist. We then discussed the result in order to arrive at a common view.

5 Testing

First we did some initial experimenting with a preliminary test sample in order to tune the parameters. We then clustered the corpus data and evaluated the clusters against the gold standard, which gave an estimate of the synonym content of the clusters. In addition, we performed a manual evaluation of the result of the

Clustering method	Information radius		Cosine distance		Euclidean distance	
	R	P	R	P	R	P
Average link	47	42	43	41	43	41
Complete link	47	40	42	39	42	38
K-means	-	-	43	36	42	36
SOM	-	-	-	-	41	35

Table 3: Cluster synonym content as average recall (R) and precision (P) in per cent (%) with a standard deviation of 2 % using different clustering methods and similarity measures.

Clustering method	Cosine distance w rotated feature space		Cosine distance w/o rotation	
	R	P	R	P
Average link	43	41	42	32
Complete link	42	39	41	33

Table 4: Cluster synonym content as average recall (R) and precision (P) in per cent (%) with a standard deviation of 2 % using a denoised and a noisy low-dimensional feature space.

best clustering algorithm.

5.1 Parameter selection

We clustered the words in L_w with the complete-link and average-link clustering algorithms using the dis_w similarity information. The algorithms form hierarchical cluster trees which need to be split into clusters at some level. The inconsistency coefficient c characterizes each link in a cluster tree by comparing its length with the average size of other links at the same level of the hierarchy. The higher the value of this coefficient, the less similar the objects connected by the link (The MathWorks, Inc., 2002). We selected the inconsistency coefficient $c = 1$ by testing on a separate initial test set different from the final evaluation data.

Using the cosine distance $cosd(p_{w,T}, q_{w,T})$ as a similarity measure on the projected and rotated representation of the words we clustered with the above mentioned standard clustering algorithms as well as with the k-means algorithm. Using the euclidean distance $eucld(p_{w,T}, q_{w,T})$ we also produced self-organizing maps (SOM). For k-means and SOM an initial number of clusters need to be selected. We selected 35 clusters as this was close to the average of what the other algorithms produced, which we were comparing with. For k-means we used the best out of 10 iterations and for SOM we trained a 5×7 hexagonal gridtop for 10 epochs. We also tried a considerably longer training period for SOM but noticed only an insignificant improvement on the cluster precision.

We also tried a number of other algorithms in the MATLAB package, but they typically produced a result either containing only the word itself or clusters containing more than one fifth of the words in the key cluster. We deemed such clustering results a failure on our data without need for formal evaluation.

5.2 Experiments

After evaluating against the translation dictionary gold standard, the result of the experiment with complete-link, average-link, k-means and SOM clustering using different similarity measures is shown in Table 3. *The best recall with the best precision was achieved with the average-link clustering using the information radius on the original feature space* with $47 \pm 2\,\%$ recall and and $42 \pm 2\,\%$ precision. This produced clusters with an average size of 6.05 words.

The difference between complete-link and average-link clustering is not statistically significant even if the average-link is slightly better. *The recall is statistically significantly better in the original feature space than in the low-dimensional space at the risk level $p = 0.05$, whereas the precision remains roughly the same.* The average-link and complete-link clustering have a statistically significantly better precision than k-means and SOM, respectively, at the risk level $p < 0.05$. We can also see that there is hardly any difference in practice between the Euclidean distance on normalized word vectors and the cosine distance despite the fact that the centroids were not normalized when using the squared Euclidean distance with k-means.

As can be seen from Table 4 the rotation of the low-dimensional feature space using SVD has the effect of increasing precision statistically significantly at the risk level $p < 0.005$, i.e. the

Word	alijäämä/deficit	maatalous/agriculture	tuki/aid
Synonymy	vaje/deficiency vajaus/shortfall		avustus/subsidy apu/help
Antonymy	ylijäämä/surplus		
Complementarity		teollisuus/industry vientiteollisuus/export industry elintarviketeollisuus/food industry	
Hyperonymy		elinkeinoelämä/business talouselämä/economy	
Hyponymy			rahoitus/financing

Table 5: Semantic relations of the cluster content of some sample words (English glosses added)

Content Relations	Dictionary sample	All words sample
Synonymy	52 %	38 %
Antonymy	1 %	1 %
Complementarity	12 %	34 %
Hyperonymy	2 %	4 %
Hyponymy	1 %	3 %
Other	31 %	21 %
Total	100 %	100 %

Table 6: Manual evaluation of the percentage of different semantic relations in the cluster content in two different samples of 50 clusters each.

clusters become less noisy.

We then performed a manual evaluation of the output of the best clustering algorithm. We used one cluster sample from the 453 clusters qualifying for mechanical evaluation and one sample from the whole set of 1753 clusters. The results of the manual evaluation is shown in Table 6. The evaluation shows that 69-79 % of the material in the clusters is relevant for constructing a thesaurus.

The manual evaluation agrees with the mechanical evaluation, when the manual evaluation found a synonym content of 52 %, compared to the minimum synonym content of 42 % found by the mechanical evaluation. This means that the clusters actually contain a few more synonyms than those conservatively agreed on by the three translation dictionaries.

If we evaluate the sample of key clusters drawn from all the words in the test sample, we get a synonym content of 38 %. This figure is rather low, but can be explained by the fact that many of the words were compound nouns that had no synonyms, which is why the translation dictionaries either did not have them listed or contained no additional source word synonyms for them.

In Table 5, we see a few sample clusters whose words we rated during manual evaluation.

6 Discussion

The feature selection and the feature weighting radically influences the outcome of the results of any machine learning task. This has been noted in several evaluations of supervised machine learning algorithms (Voorhees et al., 1995; Yarowsky and Florian, 2002; Lindén, 2003). During clustering, i.e. unsupervised learning, the features extracted from the corpus are the only information guiding the machine learning in addition to the clustering principle, which makes successful feature extraction, good feature weighting and accurate similarity measurements crucial for the success of the clustering. The clustering algorithms only exploit and preserve the information provided by the features and the similarity measure.

In (Weeds, 2003; Lee, 2001; Dagan et al., 1999), the information radius is applied to find words that can be used as distributional proxies for one another. They extract features only from verb relations whereas we use the full range of dependency syntactic relations. One intention of this study was to evaluate whether the selected corpus and the features extracted provide a basis for forming linguistically meaningful clusters that are useful in thesaurus construction. The result showed that 69-79 % of the words found in the key clusters are useful, which is very encouraging. It turned out that the chosen features as such were useful, even if the over-all result probably could benefit from a more nuanced feature weighting scheme. We do not yet fully understand how the initial feature weighting affects the outcome of the clustering. Perhaps there are features that would contribute to a more fine-grained clustering if properly weighted.

Next we intend to identify more than a single key cluster for each word, which poses additional challenges for the evaluation. We also aim at evaluating the generated clusters in an information retrieval setting in order to see if they improve performance despite the fact that they contain more than synonyms. This would also shed some light on exactly how much synonymy we need to aim at in a practical application.

7 Conclusion

We have demonstrated that it is feasible to calculate similarities between words using a full dependency syntactic feature space. We have also introduced similarity recalculation during clustering as a fast approximation of the high-dimensional feature space. In addition we introduced a way to use translation dictionaries for evaluating the rate of synonymy found in the word clusters, which is useful for languages that do not yet have publicly available thesaurus resources like WordNet. Finally we have shown that 69-79 % of the words in the discovered clusters are useful for thesaurus construction.

Acknowledgements

The second author made the Jensen-Shannon similarity lists and the corpus processing described in Sections 2, 3.1 and 3.2, and the first author did the rest. We are grateful to Lauri Carlson, Kimmo Koskenniemi and Mathias Creutz for helpful comments on the manuscript and to Juhani Jokinen for manually evaluating the test samples.

References

Connexor. 2002. Machinese phrase tagger. [http://www.connexor.com/].

James Richard Curran. 2003. *From Distributional to Semantic Similarity*. Ph.D. thesis, Institute for Communicating and Collaborative Systems, School of Informatics, University of Edinburgh.

Ido Dagan, Lillian Lee, and Fernando C. N. Pereira. 1999. Similarity-based models of word co-occurrence probabilities. *Machine Learning*, 34(1–3):43–69.

Christiane Fellbaum. 1998. *WordNet, An Electronic Lexical Database*. The MIT Press.

Zellig Harris. 1968. Mathematical structures of language. *Interscience Tracts in Pure and Applied Mathematics*, 21(ix):230 pp.

A. K. Jain, M. N. Murty, and P. J. Flynn. 1999. Data clustering: a review. *ACM Computing Surveys*, 31(3):264–323.

Kielikone. 2004. Dictionary service mot - dictionaries and terminologies. [http://www.kielikone.fi/en/].

Teuvo Kohonen. 1997. *Self-Organizing Maps (Second Edition)*, volume 30 of *Springer Series in Information Sciences*. Springer, Berlin.

Lillian Lee. 1999. Measures of distributional similarity. In *37th Annual Meeting of the Association for Computational Linguistics*, pages 25–32.

Lillian Lee. 2001. On the effectiveness of the skew divergence for statistical language analysis. In *Artificial Intelligence and Statistics 2001*, pages 65–72.

Jianhua Lin. 1991. Divergence measures based on the Shannon entropy. *IEEE Transactions on Information Theory*, 37(1):145–151, January.

Krister Lindén. 2003. Word sense disambiguation with thessom. In *Proceedings of the WSOM'03 – Intelligent Systems and Innovational Computing*, Kitakuyshu, Japan, September.

Christopher D. Manning and Hinrich Schütze. 1999. *Foundations of Statistical Natural Language Processing*. The MIT Press, Cambridge, Massachusetts.

Patrick André Pantel. 2003. *Clustering by Committee*. Ph.D. thesis, University of Alberta, Edmonton, Alberta, Canada.

The MathWorks, Inc. 2002. Matlab with statistics toolbox and neural network toolbox. [http://www.mathworks.com/], June 18. Version 6.5.0.180913a Release 13.

Ellen M. Voorhees, Claudia Leacock, and Geoffrey Towell, 1995. *Computational Learning Theory and Natural Language Learning Systems 3: Selecting Good Models*, chapter Learning context to disambiguate word senses, pages 279–305. MIT Press, Cambridge.

Piek Vossen. 2001. Eurowordnet. [http://www.hum.uva.nl/~ewn/].

Julie Elisabeth Weeds. 2003. *Measures and Applications of Lexical Distributional Similarity*. Ph.D. thesis, University of Sussex, September.

David Yarowsky and Radu Florian. 2002. Evaluating sense disambiguation across diverse parameter spaces. *Natural Language Engineering*, 8(4):293–310, December.

Term Extraction from Korean Corpora via Japanese

Atsushi Fujii, Tetsuya Ishikawa
Graduate School of Library,
Information and Media Studies
University of Tsukuba
1-2 Kasuga, Tsukuba
305-8550, Japan
{fujii,ishikawa}@slis.tsukuba.ac.jp

Jong-Hyeok Lee
Division of Electrical and
Computer Engineering,
Pohang University of Science and Technology,
Advanced Information Technology Research Center
San 31 Hyoja-dong Nam-gu,
Pohang 790-784, Republic of Korea
jhlee@postech.ac.kr

Abstract

This paper proposes a method to extract foreign words, such as technical terms and proper nouns, from Korean corpora and produce a Japanese-Korean bilingual dictionary. Specific words have been imported into multiple countries simultaneously, if they are influential across cultures. The pronunciation of a source word is similar in different languages. Our method extracts words in Korean corpora that are phonetically similar to Katakana words, which can easily be identified in Japanese corpora. We also show the effectiveness of our method by means of experiments.

1 Introduction

Reflecting the rapid growth in science and technology, new words have progressively been created. However, due to the limitation of manual compilation, new words are often out-of-dictionary words and decrease the quality of human language technology, such as natural language processing, information retrieval, machine translation, and speech recognition. To resolve this problem, a number of automatic methods to extract monolingual and bilingual lexicons from corpora have been proposed for various languages.

In this paper, we focus on extracting foreign words (or loanwords) in Korean. Technical terms and proper nouns are often imported from foreign languages and are spelled out (or transliterated) by the Korean alphabet system called *Hangul*. The similar trend can be observable in Japanese and Chinese. In Japanese, foreign words are spelled out by its special phonetic alphabet (or phonogram) called *Katakana*. Thus, foreign words can be extracted from Japanese corpora with a high accuracy, because the Katakana characters are seldom used to describe the conventional Japanese words, excepting proper nouns.

However, extracting foreign words from Korean corpora is more difficult, because in Korean both the conventional and foreign words are written with Hangul characters. This problem remains a challenging issue in computational linguistic research.

It is often the case that specific words have been imported into multiple countries simultaneously, because the source words (or concepts) are usually influential across cultures. Thus, it is feasible that a large number of foreign words in Korean can also be foreign words in Japanese.

In addition, the foreign words in Korean and Japanese corresponding to the same source word are phonetically similar. For example, the English word "system" has been imported into both Japanese and Korean. The romanized words are /`sisutemu`/ and /`siseutem`/ in both countries, respectively.

Motivated by these assumptions, we propose a method to extract foreign words in Korean corpora by means of Japanese. In brief, our method performs as follows. First, foreign words in Japanese are collected, for which Katakana words in corpora and existing lexicons can be used. Second, from Korean corpora the words that are phonetically similar to Katakana words are extracted. Finally, extracted Korean words are compiled in a lexicon with the corresponding Japanese words.

In summary, our method can extract foreign words in Korean and produce a Japanese-Korean bilingual lexicon in a single framework.

2 Methodology

2.1 Overview

Figure 1 exemplifies our extraction method, which produces a Japanese-Korean bilingual lexicon using a Korean corpus and Japanese corpus and/or lexicon. The Japanese and Korean corpora do not have to be parallel or comparable. However, it is desirable that both corpora are associated with the same domain. For the Japanese resource, the corpus and lexicon can alternatively be used or can be used together. Note that compiling Japanese monolingual lexicon is less expensive than that for a bilingual lexicon. In addition, new Katakana words can easily be extracted from a number of on-line resources, such as the World Wide Web. Thus, the use of Japanese lexicons does not decrease the utility of our method.

First, we collect Katakana words from Japanese resources. This can systematically be performed by means of a Japanese character code, such as EUC-JP and SJIS.

Second, we represent the Korean corpus and Japanese Katakana words by the Roman alphabet (i.e., romanization), so that the phonetic similarity can easily be computed. However, we use different romanization methods for Japanese and Korean.

Third, we extract candidates of foreign words from the romanized Korean corpus. An alternative method is to first perform morphological analysis on the corpus, extract candidate words based on morphemes and parts-of-speech, and romanize the extracted words. Our general model does not constrain as to which method should be used in the third step. However, because the accuracy of analysis often decreases for new words to be extracted, we experimentally adopt the former method.

Finally, we compute the phonetic similarity between each combination of the romanized Hangul and Katakana words, and select the combinations whose score is above a predefined threshold. As a result, we can obtain a Japanese-Korean bilingual lexicon consisting of foreign words.

It may be argued that English lexicons or corpora can be used as source information, instead of Japanese resources. However, because not all English words have been imported into Korean, the extraction accuracy will decrease due to extraneous words.

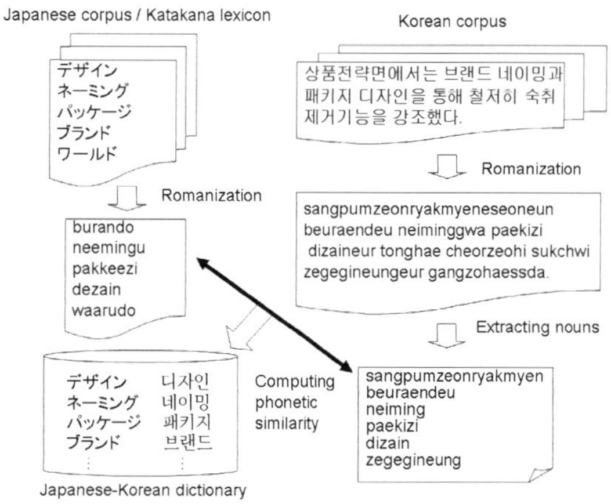

Figure 1: Overview of our extraction method.

2.2 Romanizing Japanese

Because the number of phones consisting of Japanese Katakana characters is limited, we manually produced the correspondence between each phone and its Roman representation. The numbers of Katakana characters and combined phones are 73 and 109, respectively. We also defined a symbol to represent a long vowel. In Japanese, the Hepbern and *Kunrei* systems are commonly used for romanization purposes. We use the Hepburn system, because its representation is similar to that in Korean, compared with the *Kunrei* system.

However, specific Japanese phones, such as /`ti`/, do not exist in Korean. Thus, to adapt the Hepburn system to Korean, /`ti`/ and /`tu`/ are converted to /`chi`/ and /`chu`/, respectively.

2.3 Romanizing Korean

The number of Korean Hangul characters is much greater than that of Japanese Katakana characters. Each Hangul character is a combination of more than one consonant. The pronunciation of each character is determined by its component consonants.

In Korean, there are types of consonant, i.e., the first consonant, vowel, and last consonant. The numbers of these consonants are 19, 21, and 27, respectively. The last consonant is optional. Thus, the number of combined characters is 11,172. However, to transliterate imported words, the official guideline suggests that only seven consonants be used as the last consonant. In EUC-KR, which is a standard coding system for Korean text, 2,350 common characters are coded independent of the pronunciation. Therefore, if we target corpora represented by EUC-KR, each of the 2,350 characters has to be corresponded to its Roman representation.

We use Unicode, in which Hangul characters are sorted according to the pronunciation. Figure 2 depicts a fragment of the Unicode table for Korean, in which each line corresponds to a combination of the first consonant and vowel and each column corresponds to the last consonant. The number of columns is 28, i.e., the number of the last consonants and the case in which the last consonant is not used. From this figure, the following rules can be found:

- the first consonant changes every 21 lines, which corresponds to the number of vowels,
- the vowel changes every line (i.e., 28 characters) and repeats every 21 lines,
- the last consonant changes every column.

Based on these rules, each character and its pronunciation can be identified by the three consonant types. Thus, we manually corresponded only the 68 consonants to Roman alphabets.

Figure 2: A fragment of the Unicode table for Korean Hangul characters.

We use the official romanization system for Korean, but specific Korean phones are adapted to Japanese. For example, /`j`/ and /`l`/ are converted to /`z`/ and /`r`/, respectively.

It should be noted that the adaptation is not invertible and thus is needed for both J-to-K and K-to-J directions.

For example, the English word "cheese", which has been imported to both Korean and Japanese as a foreign word, is romanized as /`chiseu`/ in Korean and /`ti:zu`/ in Japanese. Here, /`:`/ is the symbol representing a Japanese long vowel. Using the adaptation, these expressions are converted to /`chizu`/ and /`chi:zu`/, respectively, which look more similar to each other, compared with the original strings.

2.4 Extracting term candidates from Korean corpora

To extract candidates of foreign words from a Korean corpus, we first extract phrases. This can be performed systematically, because Korean sentences are segmented on a phrase-by-phrase basis.

Second, because foreign words are usually nouns, we use hand-crafted rules to remove post-position suffixes (e.g., *Josa*) and extract nouns from phrases.

Third, we discard nouns including the last consonants that are not recommended for transliteration purposes in the official guideline. Although the guideline suggests other rules for transliteration, existing foreign words in Korean are not necessarily regulated by these rules.

Finally, we consult a dictionary to discard existing Korean words, because our purpose is to extract new words. For this purpose, we experimentally use the dictionary for SuperMorph-K morphological analyzer[1], which includes approximately 50,000 Korean words.

2.5 Computing Similarity

Given romanized Japanese and Korean words, we compute the similarity between the two strings and select the pairs associated with the score above a threshold as translations. We use a DP (dynamic programming) matching method to identify the number of differences (i.e., insertion, deletion, and substitution) between two strings, on a alphabet-by-alphabet basis.

In principle, if two strings are associated with a smaller number of differences, the similarity between them becomes greater. For this purpose, a Dice-style coefficient can be used.

However, while the use of consonants in transliteration is usually the same across languages, the use of vowels can vary significantly depending on the language. For example, the English word "system" is romanized as /`sisutemu`/ and /`siseutem`/ in Japanese and Korean, respectively. Thus, the differences in consonants between two strings should be penalized more than the differences in vowels.

In view of the above discussion, we compute the similarity between two romanized words by Equation (1).

$$1 - \frac{2 \cdot (\alpha \cdot dc + dv)}{\alpha \cdot c + v} \quad (1)$$

Here, dc and dv denote the numbers of differences in consonants and vowels, respectively, and α is a parametric constant used to control the importance of the consonants. We experimentally set $\alpha = 2$. In addition, c and v denote the numbers of all consonants and vowels in the two strings. The similarity ranges from 0 to 1.

3 Experimentation

3.1 Evaluating Extraction Accuracy

We collected 111,166 Katakana words (word types) from multiple Japanese lexicons, most of which were technical term dictionaries.

We used the Korean document set in the NTCIR-3 Cross-lingual Information Retrieval test collection[2]. This document set consists of 66,146 newspaper articles of Korean Economic Daily published in 1994. We randomly selected 50 newspaper articles and used them for our experiment. We asked a graduate student excluding the authors of this paper to identify foreign words in the target text. As a result, 124 foreign word types (205 word tokens) were identified, which were less than we had expected. This was partially due to the fact that newspaper articles generally do not contain a large number of foreign words, compared with technical publications.

We manually classified the extracted words and used only the words that were imported to both Japan and Korea from other languages. We discarded foreign words in Korea imported from Japan, because these words were often spelled out by non-Katakana characters, such as Kanji (Chinese character). A sample of these words includes "*Tokyo* (the capital of Japan)", "*Heisei* (the current Japanese era name)", and "*enko* (personal connection)". In addition, we discarded the foreign proper nouns for which the human subject was not able to identify the source word. As a result, we obtained 67 target word types. Examples of original English words for these words are as follows:

> digital, group, dollar, re-engineering, line, polyester, Asia, service, class, card, computer, brand, liter, hotel.

Thus, our method can potentially be applied to roughly a half of the foreign words in Korean text.

We used the Japanese words to extract plausible foreign words from the target Korean corpus. We first romanized the corpus and extracted nouns by removing post-position suffixes. As a result, we obtained 3,106 words including all the 67 target words. By discarding the words in the dictionary for SuperMorph-K, 958 words including 59 target words were remained.

For each of the remaining 958 words, we computed the similarity between each of the 111,166 Japanese words. For evaluation purposes, we varied a threshold for the similarity and investigated the relation between precision and recall. Recall is the ratio of the number of target foreign words extracted by our method and the total number of target foreign

[1] http://www.omronsoft.com/

[2] http://research.nii.ac.jp/ntcir/index-en.html

words. Precision is the ratio of the number of target foreign words extracted by our method and the total number of words obtained by our method.

Table 1 shows the precision and recall for different methods. While we varied a threshold of a similarity, we also varied the number of Korean words corresponded to a single Katakana word (N). By decreasing the value of the threshold and increasing the number of words extracted, the recall can be improved but the precision decreases. In Table 1, the precision and recall are in an extreme trade-off relation. For example, when the recall was 69.5%, the precision was only 1.2%.

We manually analyzed the words that were not extracted by our method. Out of the 59 target words, 12 compound words consisting of both conventional and foreign words were not extracted. However, our method extracted compound words consisting of only foreign words. In addition, the three words that did not have counterparts in the input Japanese words were not extracted.

Table 1: Precision/Recall for term extraction.

	Threshold for similarity		
	>0.9	>0.7	>0.5
N=1	50.0/8.5	12.7/40.7	4.1/47.5
N=10	50.0/8.5	7.4/47.5	1.2/69.5

3.2 Application-Oriented Evaluation

During the first experiment, we determined a specific threshold value for the similarity between Katakana and Hangul words and selected the pairs whose similarity was above the threshold. As a result, we obtained 667 Korean words, which were used to enhance the dictionary for the SuperMorph-K morphological analyzer.

We performed morphological analysis on the 50 articles used in the first experiment, which included 1,213 sentences and 9,557 word tokens. We also investigated the degree to which the analytical accuracy is improved by means of the additional dictionary. Here, accuracy is the ratio of the number of correct word segmentations and the total segmentations generated by SuperMorph-K. The same human subject as in the first experiment identified the correct word segmentations for the input articles.

First, we focused on the accuracy of segmenting foreign words. The accuracy was improved from 75.8% to 79.8% by means of the additional dictionary. The accuracy for all words was changed from 94.6% to 94.8% by the additional dictionary.

In summary, the additional dictionary was effective for analyzing foreign words and was not associated with side effect for the overall accuracy. At the same time, we concede that we need larger-scale experiments to draw firmer conclusions.

4 Related Work

A number of corpus-based methods to extract bilingual lexicons have been proposed (Smadja et al., 1996). In general, these methods use statistics obtained from a parallel or comparable bilingual corpus and extract word or phrase pairs that are strongly associated with each other. However, our method uses a monolingual Korean corpus and a Japanese lexicon independent of the corpus, which can easily be obtained, compared with parallel or comparable bilingual corpora.

Jeong et al. (1999) and Oh and Choi (2001) independently explored a statistical approach to detect foreign words in Korean text. Although the detection accuracy is reasonably high, these methods require a training corpus in which conventional and foreign words are annotated. Our approach does not require annotated corpora, but the detection accuracy is not high enough as shown in Section 3.1. A combination of both approaches is expected to compensate the drawbacks of each approach.

5 Conclusion

We proposed a method to extract foreign words, such as technical terms and proper nouns, from Korean corpora and produce a Japanese-Korean bilingual dictionary. Specific words, which have been imported into multiple countries, are usually spelled out by special phonetic alphabets, such as Katakana in Japanese and Hangul in Korean.

Because extracting foreign words spelled out by Katakana in Japanese lexicons and corpora can be performed with a high accuracy, our method extracts words in Korean corpora that are phonetically similar to Japanese Katakana words. Our method does not require parallel or comparable bilingual corpora and human annotation for these corpora.

We also performed experiments in which we extracted foreign words from Korean newspaper articles and used the resultant dictionary for morphological analysis. We found that our method did not correctly extract compound Korean words consisting of both conventional and foreign words. Future work includes larger-scale experiments to further investigate the effectiveness of our method.

References

Kil Soon Jeong, Sung Hyon Myaeng, Jae Sung Lee, and Key-Sun Choi. 1999. Automatic identification and back-transliteration of foreign words for information retrieval. *Information Processing & Management*, 35:523–540.

Jong-Hoon Oh and Key sun Choi. 2001. Automatic extraction of transliterated foreign words using hidden markov model. In *Proceedings of ICCPOL-2001*, pages 433–438.

Frank Smadja, Kathleen R. McKeown, and Vasileios Hatzivassiloglou. 1996. Translating collocations for bilingual lexicons: A statistical approach. *Computational Linguistics*, 22(1):1–38.

Quantitative Portraits of Lexical Elements

Kyo Kageura
Human and Social Information Research Division
National Institute of Informatics,
2-1-2 Hitotsubashi, Chiyoda-ku,
Tokyo, 101-8430, Japan
kyo@nii.ac.jp

Abstract

This paper clarifies the basic concepts and theoretical perspectives by and from which quantitative "weighting" of lexical elements are defined, and then draws, quantitative portraits of a few lexical elements in order to exemplify the relevance of the concepts and perspectives examined.

1 Introduction

Since Luhn's pioneering work (Luhn, 1958) in automatic term weighting, many methods have been proposed in the fields of IR (e.g. Spark-Jones, 1973; Harter, 1975) and NLP (e.g. Church et al., 1990). Some "standard" methods of term weighting such as $tfidf$ have been established (Aizawa, 2003; 徳永, 1999) and the application range has widened; term weighting has become a mature technology.

Despite this, what has been technically proposed has not been examined from a theoretical point of view, i.e. what kind of weighting scheme reflects what kind of lexical nature within what kind of framework of interpretations in language. We will clarify this and then illustrate the relevance of this clarification by drawing quantitative portraits of some lexical items using the quantitative measures.

2 Texts and lexica

Automatic term weighting starts from texts/documents. To what spheres the weights are attributed can differ. Figure 1 shows the linguistic spheres of lexica and texts (Kageura, 2002); there are both concrete data spheres and abstract spheres on both the lexical and textual sides.

Within this scheme, three types of relations between lexica and texts can be identified: concrete terms attributed to concrete texts, concrete terms corresponding to discourse, and abstract lexica corresponding to abstract discourse. We will show below that three major types of automatic term weighting methods correspond to these three types of relations between lexica and texts.

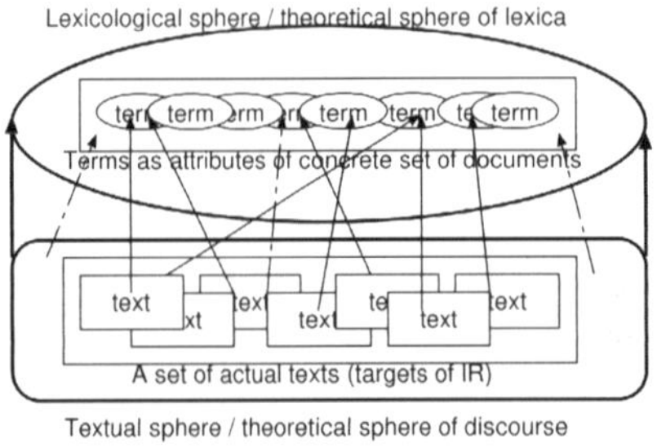

Figure 1: Textual sphere and lexicological sphere.

3 Methods of term weighting

3.1 Tfidf

$Tfidf$ is defined as:

$$tfidf = f_{t_i} \log \frac{N}{N_i} \qquad (1)$$

where f_{t_i} is the total frequency of a term t_i, N is the total number of the documents, and N_i is the total number of documents in which the term t_i occurs.

Aizawa (2003) has shown that this can be derived from an information theoretic measure. Let $\mathcal{D}$ and $\mathcal{T}$ be random variables defined over events in a set of documents $D = \{d_1, d_2, ..., d_i, ..., d_N\}$ and a set of different terms $T = \{t_1, t_2, ..., t_j, ..., t_M\}$ in D. Let f_{ij} denote the frequency of t_i in d_j, f_{w_i} the total frequency of t_i, f_{d_j} the total number of running terms in d_j, and F the total number of term tokens in D. The "weight" of a term t_i can be given by:

$$\begin{aligned} \mathcal{F}(t_i; \mathcal{D}) &= P(t_i)\, \mathcal{K}(P(\mathcal{D}|t_i)||P(\mathcal{D})) \\ &= P(t_i) \sum_{d_j \in D} P(d_j|t_i) \log \frac{P(d_j|t_i)}{P(d_j)} \end{aligned}$$

Giving probabilities by relative frequencies, and assuming that all the documents have equal size and the frequency of t_i in the documents that contain t_i is equal, this measure becomes $tfidf$; $tfidf$ has an information theoretic meaning *within the given set of documents* (Figure 2).

3.2 Term representativeness

Hisamitsu, et al. (2000a) proposed a measure of "term representativeness", in order to overcome the

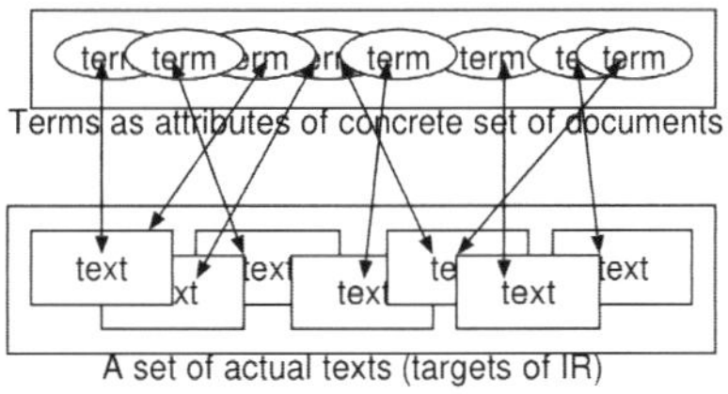

Figure 2: The position of $tfidf$.

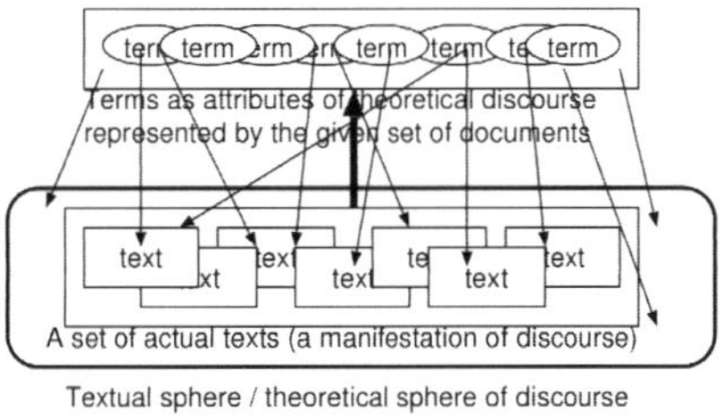

Figure 3: The position of term representativeness.

excessive sensitivity of weighting measures to token frequencies. They hypothesised that, for a term t, if the term is representative, D_t (the set of all documents containing t) have some specific characteristic. They define a measure which calculates the distance between a distributional characteristic of words around t and the same distributional characteristic in the whole document set.

In order to remove the factor of data size dependency, Hisamitsu et al. (2000a) defines the "baseline function," which indicates the distance between the distribution of words in the original document set and the distribution of words in randomly selected document subsets for each size. The distance between the distribution of words in the original document set and the distribution of words in the documents which accompany the focal term t is normalised by the "baseline function."

Formally,

$$Rep(t) = \frac{Dist(P_t, P)}{Dist(P_{R_t}, P)} \quad (2)$$

where D denotes the set of all documents; P the distribution of words in D; t a focal term; D_t the set of all documents containing t; P_t distribution of words in D_t; P_{R_t} distribution of words in randomly selected documents whose size equals D_t; $Dist(P_i, P_j)$ the distance between two distributions of words P_i and P_j. Log-likelihood ratio was used to measure the distance.

This measure observes the centripetal force of a term vis-à-vis discourse. i.e. *it captures the characteristic of terms in the general discourse as represented by the given set of documents* (Figure 3).

3.3 Lexical productivity

Nakagawa (2000) incorporates a factor of lexical productivity of constituent elements of compound

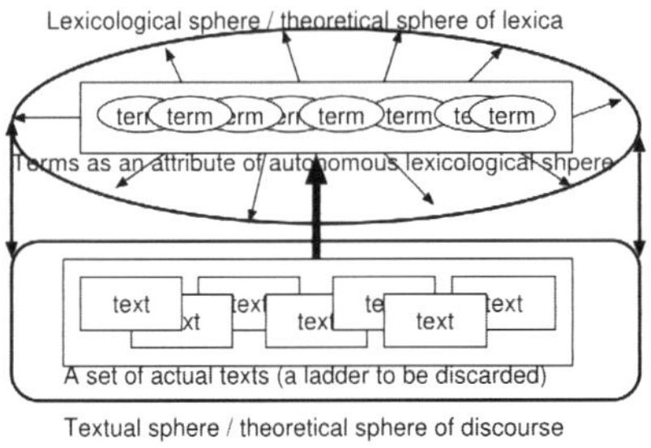

Figure 4: The position of lexical productivity.

units for complex term extraction. The method observes in how many different compounds an element t_i is used in a given document set (let us denote this as $d(i, N)$ where N indicates the size of the overall document set as counted by the number of word tokens), and used that in the weighting of compounds containing t_i, by taking weighted average. By explicitly limiting the syntagmatic range of observation of cooccurrence *to the unit of compounds*, he focused on the lexical productivity as manifasted in texts.

This measure depends on the token occurrence, but we can also think of the *theoretical* lexical productivity in the lexicological sphere: how many compounds t_i can *potentially* make" (let us denote this by $d(i)$). For that, it is necessary to remove the factor of token occurrence. This can be done by:

$$d(i) = d(i, \lambda N) \quad (\lambda \to \infty).$$

This has so far been unexplored. Potential lexical productivity of an element can be estimated from textual data: Letting p_{t_i} be the occurrence probability of t_i in texts, $f(i, N)$ be the token occurrence of t_i in texts, and C_i be the sample space $\{i_1, i_2, i_3, ..., i_{d(i)}\}$ of the distribution of compounds (and simplex word) that contains t_i with probability $p_{(c)_{i_k}}$ given to each compound i_k, and assuming the combination of binomial distribution, we have:

$$\begin{aligned} \mathrm{E}[f(i,N)] &= p_{t_i} \cdot N \\ \mathrm{E}[d(i,N)] &= \sum_{m=1}^{p_{t_i} \cdot N} \sum_{k=1}^{d(i)} \binom{p_{t_i} \cdot N}{m} p_{i_k}^m (1 - p_{i_k})^{1-m}. \end{aligned}$$

What is given in the data is the empirical value for $d(i, N)$, with the empirical distributions of what actually occur in the document set among C_i. $d(i)$ can be estimated by LNRE methods (Baayen, 2001).

Being a measure representing the potential power of a lexical element t_i for constructing compounds, $d(i)$ indicates *the lexical productivity in the lexicological sphere* which correspond to theoretical sphere of discourse as represented by the given document set (Figure 4).

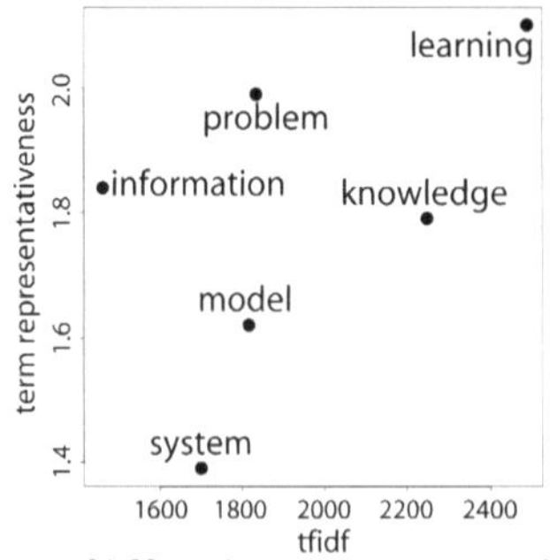

Figure 5: *tfidf* and term representativeness.

4 Portraits of lexical elements

As the three different measures capture three different aspects of lexical elements, they are not competitive [1]. We here use these measures to illustrate characteristics of a few lexical elements.

We used NII morphologically tagged-corpus for observation (Okada et al., 2001), which consists of Japanese abstracts in the field of artificial intelligence. Table 1 shows the basic quantitative information.

No. of abstracts	word tokens (simplex/compound)	word types (simp./comp.)
1816	299846/230708	8764/23243

Table 1: The basic data for NII corpus.

We chose the six most frequently occurring nominal element for observation, i.e. システム (system), 知識 (knowledge), 学習 (learning), 問題 (problem), モデル (model), and 情報 (information). Intuitively, "system", and "model" are rather general with respect to the domain of artificial intelligence, "knowledge" and "learning" are domain specific, and "information" and "problem" are in between. Table 2 shows the basic quantitative information for these six lexical elements.

Figure 5 plots *tfidf* and term representativeness for the six elements. Table 3 shows the estimated value of lexical productivity.

	p	$d(i)$
system	0.96	273402688337
knowledge	0.88	689
learning	0.39	2251563675
problem	0.70	1951
model	0.47	3676671255
information	0.84	667

Table 3: Lexical productivity for the six elements.

Figure 5 shows "learning" and "knowledge", intuitively the domain-dependent elements, take high *tfidf* values, while "information" takes the lowest value. Term representativeness gives "learning" a high value but the values of "knowledge" is much lower, and about the same as "information". Interestingly, the lexical productivity of "knowledge" and "information" is also very close to each other.

It is possible to infer from these values of term representativeness and lexical productivity that both "information" and "knowledge" are, within the discourse of artificial intelligence, not with high centripetal value as both are rather "base" concepts of the domain. If we observe Table 2, "knowledge" is more often used as it is, while "information" tends to occur as compounds. From this we might be able to hypothesise that "knowledge" is in itself the "base" concept of artificial intelligence while "information" becomes the "base" concept in combination with other lexical items. This fits our intuition, as "information" in itself is more a "base" concept of information and computer science, which is a broader domain of which artificial intelligence is a subdomain. The low *tfidf* value of "information" comes from the low token frequency coupled with relatively high DF, which shows that "information", as long as it is used, tends to scatter across documents. This is in accordance with the interpretation that "information" tends to occur in compounds. Still, however, it is difficult to interpret sensibly the fact that the *tfidf* value of "information" is lower than those of "model" and "system". Perhaps it is more sensible to interpret *tfidf* among elements which take the values of term representativeness higher than a certain threshold. Then we can say that "learning" and "knowledge" represent concepts more "central" to the domain of artificial intelligence than "information".

The element "learning", which takes the highest values both in *tfidf* and in term representativeness, is conspicuous in its lexical productivity. Compared to "knowledge" whose *tfidf* value is also high, and with the three elements "problem", "information" and "knowledge" whose term representativeness values are relatively high, the order of lexical productivity of "learning" is a million times higher (and similar to "model" or "system"). Table 2 shows that "learning" does not occur much as it is, nor does it occur much as the head of compounds. This indicates that "learning" represents an important concept of the given data and in the discourse of artificial intelligence, but only "indirectly" in combination with other elements in compounds where "learning" tend to contribute to as a modifier rather than a head.

The two "general" lexical elements, i.e. "model"

[1] It is thus simplistic to evaluate which measures work better in an application, unless the conceptual status of the applications is sufficiently clarified.

	TF	DF	Comp(A)	Comp(H)	Simp	$d(i,N)$(A)	$d(i,N)$(H)
system	2659	989	1922	1247	737	937	502
knowledge	2183	669	1399	443	784	424	137
learning	1776	462	1513	208	263	375	73
problem	1758	660	1197	558	561	334	152
model	1480	550	1144	687	343	447	263
information	1038	460	656	268	382	207	155

Note: Comp(A) indicates the number of compounds that contains the lexical element; Comp(H) indicates the number of compounds that contains the lexical element as the head; $d(i,N)$(A) indicates the number of different compounds (plus one simplex) that contains the lexical element; $d(i,N)$(H) indicates the number of different compounds (plus one simplex) that contains the lexical element as the head.

Table 2: The basic data for the six lexical elements.

and "system", take low term representativeness values[2]. This is in accordance with our intuition. The lexical productivity of these two elements are extremely high (practically infinite). This indicates that these two elements can be widely used in varieties of discoursal contexts, without in itself contributing much to consolidating the content of discourse. This fits nicely to our intuitive interpretation of the meanings of these two elements, i.e. they are orthogonal to to such domain-dependent elements as "knowledge" or "learning".

This leaves us with the final element "problem". The value of term representativeness is high, second only to "learning" and in between "learning" and "information"/"knowledge". The lexical productivity is much closer to "information" and "knowledge" than to the other three. As such, "problem" can be interpreted as a kind of "base" concept, though it retains stronger centripetal force than "information" and "knowledge". If we ignore $tfidf$ values of "model" and "system" and only compare "information", "problem", "learning" and "knowledge", it is also sensible to see that "problem" represent a concept more central to the domain than "information" but less central than "learning" and "knowledge".

5 Conclusions

We have shown that different term weighting measures have different spheres of interpretation; on the basis of that we have illustrated that the combination of these can illustrates complex aspects of lexical nature. Though it can be argued that the present study does not show ways for applications nor "empirical" evaluations within applications, we believe that "empirical" evaluations should be properly founded by the framework of interpretation in order for the results to be generalised in a scientific way; history of sciences have shown that often reliance on "empirical" evaluations correlates with the lack of theory or scientific wholesomeness.

[2]This is in accordance with the observation by Hisamitsu et al. (2000) which says that the measure of term representativeness is particularly useful to exclude general elements.

References

Akiko N. Aizawa. 2003. An information-theoretic perspective of tf-idf measures. *Information Processing and Management*, 39(1): 45–65.

Harald Baayen. 2001. *Word Frequency Distributions*. Dordrecht: Kluwer.

Kenneth W. Church and Patrick Hanks. 1990. Word association norms, mutual information and lexicography. *Computational Linguistics*, 16(1): 22–29.

S. P. Harter. 1975. A probabilistic approach to automatic keyword indexing. *Journal of the American Society for Information Science*, 26(4): 197–206.

Toru Hisamitsu, et. al. 2000. A method of measuring term representativeness. *COLING 2000*, 320–326.

Kyo Kageura. 2002. *The Dynamics of Terminology*. Amsterdam: John Benjamins.

Hans P. Luhn. 1958. The automatic creation of literature abstracts. *IBM Journal of Research and Development*, 2(2): 159–165.

Hiroshi Nakagawa. 2000. Automatic term recognition based on statistics of compound nouns. *Terminology*, 6(2): 195–210.

Maho Okada, et. al. 2001. Defining principled but practically manageable lexical units in Japanese textual corpora. *NLPRS'01 Workshop on Language Resources in Asia*, 47–53.

Karen Sparck-Jones. 1973. Index term weighting. *Information Storage and Retrieval*, 9(11): 619–633.

徳永健伸. 1999. **情報検索と言語処理**. 東京: 東大出版会.

Term Extraction Using Verb Co-occurrence

Teruo KOYAMA and Kyo KAGEURA
Human and Social Information Research, National Institute of Informatics
2-1-2, Hitotsubashi, Chiyoda-ku
101-8430, Tokyo
Japan
{t_koyama,kyo}@nii.ac.jp

Abstract

This paper proposes a method of automatic term extraction in which documents are grouped on the basis of discourse/domains by means of characteristic verbs and nominal terms. The method aims to (a) extract terms in accordance with their general positions in the discourse, (b) enhance the precision of extraction and (c) cover relatively low-frequency terms in extraction. Experiments show that it performs well in terms of these objectives.

1 Introduction

Term extraction is important in natural language processing, especially in addressing the lexical bottleneck. To date, various statistical methods, such as TF-IDF, have been applied to this task, and have attained great success (Aizawa, 2003; Bourigault et al., 1998; Daille et al., 1994; Kageura & Koyama, 2000; Mima & Ananiadou, 2000; Moens, 2000; Nakagawa, 2000).

However, some problems still remain: (a) the concept of "domain" or "field" is determined mostly in advance; (b) the positions of extracted terms in the domain are not very clear; (c) generally, in statistical approaches, the results are sensitive to frequency, and it is difficult to deal with low-frequency terms.

This paper proposes a way of dealing with these problems. The basic idea is that there are some characteristic verbs used in scientific discourse, which can be used (a) to define the domains/sub-domains in the corpora of the broad domain and (b) to estimate the positions[1] of terms that co-occur with them using clustering analysis.

Some studies have analyzed the role of verbs in documents (Eumeridou et al., 2002; Klavans & Kan, 1998). Most of them focus on the microstructure of discourse, such as verb-argument relations. Our approach aims at elucidating the positions of verbs as a deciding factor in the macro discoursal structure[2] of documents in corpora.

The application of clustering in extracting various generic characteristics in language has been intensively carried out (Pereira et al., 1993; Utsuro et al., 1998). In contrast to these works, the present study is specifically concerned with macro-discourse and lexical clues that reflect it.

In the following, section 2 outlines the method we propose. Section 3 will discuss how the combination of major verbs can be used to classify terms and documents; section 4 will discuss the effect of using the proposed method in term extraction.

2 Outline of the proposed method

Our basic hypothesis is:

> For a coherent domain, sub-domain or set of documents, there are a few major "verbal" concepts and "nominal" concepts that determine the macro-structure of discourse, which are respectively represented by characteristic verbs and nouns.

Based on this hypothesis, we define the procedure of identifying macro-discourse and extracting terms as follows:

1. Extract verbs [3] and term candidates (noun related sequences) which are expected to represent macro-discourse.
2. Cluster the term candidates based on the co-occurring verbs extracted in step 1.

[1] Here, by "position", we mean to which discoursal class, sub-domain or conceptual group a term belongs. See Sowa (1993) for some related discussion about the position of concepts represented in terms.

[2] By "macro" we mean the generalized discoursal structure that characterizes a domain, a sub-domain or a group of documents.

[3] Here, we include verb stems as well according to Japanese word classification.

3. Manually identify groups of term candidates that correspond to macro-discourse groups, and identify representative vectors consisting of verbs that correspond to discoursal groups on the basis of step 2.
4. Cluster documents on the basis of verb vectors defined in step 3.
5. For each clustered document, apply a basic term extraction method.

By identifying discourse groups within given corpora, it is possible to macro-structurize terms. Also, quantitative information is expected to become relatively more sensitive to low-frequency term candidates.

In the following experiments, we use a corpus extracted from the database edited by NII (National Institute of Informatics), consisting of research reports in various scientific fields supported by grant-in-aid from the Japan Society for the Promotion of Science for 1998. We use two sub-corpora, i.e. in the field of engineering and in natural science.

The number of reports is 7753 for engineering and 5171 for natural science. Each report consists of about 750 (Japanese) characters.

We applied the "Juman" morphological analyzer and extracted sequences of nouns or word stems as (noun) term candidates.

3 Defining contextual information

Here, we elaborate on steps 1 to 3 described in section 2.

Step#1.

First, we order candidate terms and verbs by TF-IDF, in order to select important terms and verbs in the domain. We select the 15 verbs and 50 candidate terms with the highest TF-IDF values.

Step#2.

In relation to a verb v, we can select a document set D_v which includes the verb. For this set, a parameter that indicates the strength of the co-occurrence tendency between a term t and v can be defined as

$$R_{tv} = \frac{\frac{f_v}{d_v}}{\frac{f_h}{d_h}} - 1$$

Where, [4]

[4]This parameter can be regarded to be proportional to the likelihood ratio of the appearance of t within D_v and D_h, minus one.

- f_v: term frequency in D_v
- f_h: term frequency in all documents (D_h)
- d_v: document number of D_v
- d_h: whole document number of D_h

Step#3.

Using multiple verbs, we can obtain a vector $\overrightarrow{R_t} = \{R_{tv}\}$ for the term t. Along we select 15 verbs, the 50 terms distribute themselves in a 15-dimensional vector space. On these vectors, we apply clustering analysis using the Euclidean distance and compact clustering method. Figure 1 shows the result of the analysis for the engineering corpus.

Cutting the tree at level 3, in Fig.1, we obtain 8 term groups. Each group can be presumed to be chemistry-1 (group1), material engineering (group2), civil engineering (group3), semiconductors (group4), chemistry-2 (group5), imaging (group6), system engineering/control (group7), and condensed matter physics (group8) respectively. This grouping seems to correspond to real engineering subdomains.

Applying the same method to the natural science corpus, we obtain 6 term groups, namely, chemistry-1, astronomy/geology, biology, mathematics, physics, and chemistry-2.

4 Term extraction experiment

Once the grouping of terms has been done, we can obtain mean (term) vectors for each group. These vectors can be used to evaluate the strength of the relation between a document and each term group. Suppose a vector $\overrightarrow{V_i} = \{V_{ik}\}$ is the mean vector of the i-th term group, and V_{ik} is the component corresponding to the k-th verb. The strength of the relation between a document D_j and the i-th term group is given by

$$R_{ij} = \prod_{k=1}^{n} M_{ijk} - 1$$

where,

$$M_{ijk} = \left\{ \begin{array}{ll} V_{ik} + 1 & (V_k \in T(D_j)) \\ 1 & (V_k \notin T(D_j)) \end{array} \right\}$$

$T(D_j)$ denotes the set of words in the document D_j.

Using this measure, we can apply steps 4 and 5 in section 2.

Step#4.

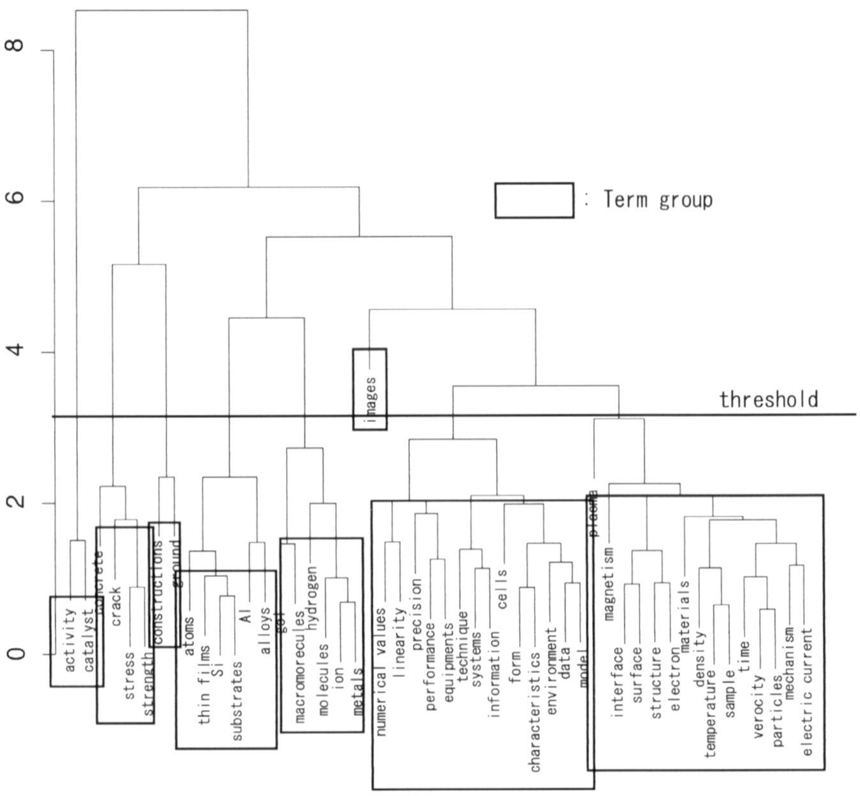

Figure 1: Result of the cluster analysis (engineering)

If we set a proper threshold, we can divide the documents into two groups, namely, documents with a (strong) relation to the term group, and others. For the engineering data, we adopt a threshold value of 0.5.

Step#5.

Once the corpus is divided into two document sets for each discoursal group, we can extract the candidates of terms, based on the division. We tried two term extraction methods. One is for rather frequent terms, and the other is for less frequent terms.

If a (frequent) candidate term has the tendency to appear more frequently in the selected document set, it can be regarded as a term belonging to the corresponding group. To evaluate the tendency, we adopt a ranking score for a candidate term C in association with term group i as

$$S_{ci} = \sqrt{f_i} \times \left(\frac{\frac{f_i}{d_i}}{\frac{f_h}{d_h}}\right)$$

Where, [5]

- f_i is the candidate term frequency in the document group i (D_i)
- f_h is the candidate term frequency in all the documents (D_h)
- d_i is the document number of D_i
- d_h is the whole document number of D_h

Less frequent terms are extracted according to the following criterion: if (i) the total frequency of a candidate is greater than or equal to 5, and (ii) over 90% of the tokens appear in the document set, then it is considered a term.

Using these methods, we can extract terms corresponding to the discoursal domain represented by term groups.

To evaluate the precision of the methods, we count the number of non-term candidates in-

[5] This value is defined as the likelihood ratio modified by the candidate frequency within the selected document group. The modification is carried out to avoid the noise caused by low-frequency candidates.

Table 1: Number of non-terms among 100 candidates (in engineering)

	documents	freq.	less-freq.
Group1	1818	9	11
Group2	2596	4	12
Group3	2078	7	8
Group4	2485	8	3
Group5	1616	10	9
Group6	1393	7	4
Group7	1326	8	8
Group8	1363	8	11
TF-IDF	-	27	
First 3800	3800	31	

cluded in the top 100 results for frequent terms, and in randomly sampled 100 results for less frequent terms.

We also prepare data on the top 100 TF-IDF value and the result of the proposed method applied to the first 3800 documents in the corpus. Table 1 shows the result.

It shows that the precision of term extraction based on document division is better than using the TF-IDF score and random grouping of documents. We applied the same method to 6 groups in the natural science field, and observed a similar improvement.

5 Conclusion and discussion

We have proposed a method of improving simple automatic term extraction based on grouping documents by discourse/domains using co-occurrences of characteristic verbs and nominal terms.

The underlying hypothesis was: If we focus on a few major "verbal" concepts and "nominal" concepts that are expected to determine the macro-structure of discourse, which are respectively represented by characteristic verbs and nouns, we could structurize or group the documents in the corpus according to the macro-structure of discourse or topic, which in turn will contribute to enhancing term extraction.

The experimental results based on the corpora, of engineering and of natural science have shown that the method is highly promising. We are currently applying the method to the corpus of human science. Though a detailed evaluation has not yet been carried out, the results so far are highly promising.

The current method still relies on some intuition and manual evaluation in the intermediate stages. We are examining ways of automatizing these phases as well as improving the methods of the term extraction phase using different weighting measures.

References

Akiko N. Aizawa. 2003. "An information-theoretic perspective of tf-idf measures," *Information Processing and Management*, 39(1): 45–65.

Bourigault, D., Jacquemin, C., and L'Homme, M. C. 1998. *Proceedings of the 1st International Workshop on Computational Terminology (Computerm 1998)*. COLING-ACL, Montreal.

Daille, B., Gaussier, E. and Langé, M. 1994. "Towards automatic extraction of monolingual and bilingual terminology," *COLING-94*: 515–521.

Eumeridou, E., Nkwenti-Azeh, B. and McNaught, J. 2002. "The contribution of verbal semantic content towards recognition," *International Journal of Corpus Linguistics*, 7(1): 87–106.

Kageura, K. and Koyama, T. eds. 2000. *Special Issue on Japanese Term Extraction: Terminology*, 6(2).

Klavans, J. and Kan, M. Y. 1998. "Role of verbs in document analysis," *COLING-ACL'98*: 680–686.

Mima, H. and Ananiadou, S. 2000. "An application and evaluation of the C/NC-value approach for the automatic term recognition of multi-word units in Japanese," *Terminology*, 6(2): 175–194.

Moens, M. F. 2000. *Automatic Indexing and Abstracting of Document Texts*. Dordrecht: Kluwer.

Nakagawa, H. 2000. "Automatic term recognition on statistics of compound nouns," *Terminology*, 6(2): 175–194.

Pereira, F., Tishby, N., and Lee, L. 1993. "Distributional clustering of English words," *ACL-92*: 128–135.

Sowa, J. F. 1993. "Lexical structures and conceptual structures." In Pustejovsky, J. ed. *Semantics and Lexicon*. Dordrecht: Kluwer. 223–262.

Utsuro, T., Miyata, T., and Matsumoto, Y. 1998. "General-to-specific model selection for subcategorization preference," *COLING-ACL'98*: 1314–1320.

Design and Implementation of a Terminology-based Literature Mining and Knowledge Structuring System

Hideki Mima
School of Engineering
University of Tokyo
Hongo 7-3-1, Bunkyo-ku, Tokyo
113-0033, Japan
mima@biz-model.t.u-tokyo.ac.jp

Sophia Ananiadou
School of Computing, Science and Engineering, University of Salford,
Salford M5 4WT, UK
National Centre for Text Mining
S.Ananiadou@salford.ac.uk

Katsumori Matsushima
School of Engineering
University of Tokyo
Hongo 7-3-1, Bunkyo-ku,
Tokyo 113-0033, Japan
matsushima@naoe.t.u-tokyo.ac.jp

Abstract

The purpose of the study is to develop an integrated knowledge management system for the domains of genome and nano-technology, in which terminology-based literature mining, knowledge acquisition, knowledge structuring, and knowledge retrieval are combined. The system supports integrating different databases (papers and patents, technologies and innovations) and retrieving different types of knowledge simultaneously. The main objective of the system is to facilitate knowledge acquisition from documents and new knowledge discovery through a terminology-based similarity calculation and a visualization of automatically structured knowledge. Implementation issues of the system are also mentioned.

Key Words: Structuring knowledge, knowledge acquisition, information extraction, natural language processing, automatic term recognition, terminology

1. Introduction

The growing number of electronically available knowledge sources (KSs) emphasizes the importance of developing flexible and efficient tools for automatic knowledge acquisition and structuring in terms of knowledge integration. Different text and literature mining techniques have been developed recently in order to facilitate efficient discovery of knowledge contained in large textual collections. The main goal of literature mining is to retrieve knowledge that is "buried" in a text and to present the distilled knowledge to users in a concise form. Its advantage, compared to "manual" knowledge discovery, is based on the assumption that automatic methods are able to process an enormous amount of texts. It is doubtful that any researcher could process such huge amount of information, especially if the knowledge spans across domains. For these reasons, literature mining aims at helping scientists in collecting, maintaining, interpreting and curating information.

In this paper, we introduce a knowledge integration and structuring system (KISS) we designed, in which terminology-driven knowledge acquisition (KA), knowledge retrieval (KR) and knowledge visualization (KV) are combined using automatic term recognition, automatic term clustering and terminology-based similarity calculation is explained. The system incorporates our proposed automatic term recognition / clustering and a visualization of retrieved knowledge based on the terminology, which allow users to access KSs visually though sophisticated GUIs.

2. Overview of the system

The main purpose of the knowledge structuring system is 1) accumulating knowledge in order to develop huge knowledge bases, 2) exploiting the accumulated knowledge efficiently. Our approach to structuring knowledge is based on:

- automatic term recognition (ATR)
- automatic term clustering (ATC) as an ontology[1] development
- ontology-based similarity calculation
- visualization of relationships among documents (KSs)

One of our definitions to structuring knowledge is discovery of relevance between documents (KSs) and its visualization. In order to achieve real time processing for structuring knowledge, we adopt terminology / ontology-based similarity calculation, because knowledge can also be represented as textual documents or passages (e.g. sentences, subsections) which are efficiently characterized by sets of specialized (technical) terms. Further details of our visualization scheme will be mentioned in Section 4.

---

[1] Although, definition of ontology is domain-specific, our definition of ontology is the collection and classification of (technical) terms to recognize their semantic relevance.

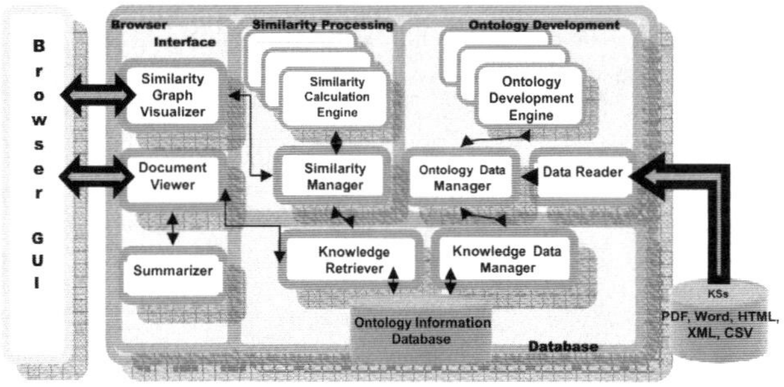

Figure 1: The system architecture

The system architecture is modular, and it integrates the following components (Figure 1):

- *Ontology Development Engine(s) (ODE)* – components that carry out the automatic ontology development which includes recognition and structuring of domain terminology;
- *Knowledge Data Manager (KDM)* – stores index of KSs and ontology in a ontology information database (OID) and provides the corresponding interface;
- *Knowledge Retriever (KR)* – retrieves KSs from TID and calculates similarities between keywords and KSs. Currently, we adopt tf*idf based similarity calculation;
- *Similarity Calculation Engine(s) (SCE)* – calculate similarities between KSs provided from KR component using ontology developed by ODE in order to show semantic similarities between each KSs. Semantic clusters of KSs are also provided.
- *Graph Visualizer* – visualizes knowledge structures based on graph expression in which relevance links between provided keywords and KSs, and relevance links between the KSs themselves can be shown.

Linguistic pre-processing within the system is performed in two steps. In the first step, POS tagging[2], i.e. the assignment of basic parts of speech (e.g. noun, verb, etc.) to words, is performed. In the second step, an ontology development engine is used to perform ATR and ATC. We also used feature structure-based parsing for English and Japanese for linguistic filter of the ATR.

3. Terminological processing as an ontology development

The lack of clear naming standards in a domain (e.g. biomedicine) makes ATR a non-trivial problem [1]. Also, it typically gives rise to many-to-many relationships between terms and concepts. In practice, two problems stem from this fact: 1) there are terms that have multiple meanings (*term ambiguity*), and, conversely, 2) there are terms that refer to the same concept (*term variation*). Generally, term ambiguity has negative effects on IE precision, while term variation decreases IE recall. These problems point out the impropriety of using simple keyword-based IE techniques. Obviously, more sophisticated techniques, identifying groups of different terms referring to the same (or similar) concept(s), and, therefore, could benefit from relying on efficient and consistent ATR/ATC and term variation management methods are required. These methods are also important for organising domain specific knowledge, as terms should not be treated isolated from other terms. They should rather be related to one another so that the relations existing between the corresponding concepts are at least partly reflected in a terminology.

Terminological processing in our system is carried out based on *C / NC-value* method [2,3] for ATR, and average mutual information based ATC (Figure 2).

3.1. Term recognition

The ATR method used in the system is based on the *C / NC-value* methods [2,3]. The *C-value* method recognizes terms by combining linguistic knowledge and statistical analysis. The method extracts multi-word terms[3] and is not limited to a specific class of concepts. It is implemented as a two-step procedure. In the first step, term candidates are extracted by using a set of linguistic filters, implemented using a LFG-based GLR parser, which describe general term formation patterns. In the second step, the term candidates are assigned termhoods (referred to as *C-values*) according to a statistical measure. The measure amalgamates four numerical corpus-based characteristics of a candidate

---

[2] We use EngCG tagger[4] in English and JUMAN / Chasen morphological analyzers in Japanese.

[3] More than 85% of domain-specific terms are multi-word terms [3].

term, namely the frequency of occurrence, the frequency of occurrence as a substring of other candidate terms, the number of candidate terms containing the given candidate term as a substring, and the number of words contained in the candidate term.

The *NC-value method* further improves the C-value results by taking into account the context of candidate terms. The relevant context words are extracted and assigned weights based on how frequently they appear with top-ranked term candidates extracted by the *C-value* method. Subsequently, context factors are assigned to candidate terms according to their co-occurrence with top-ranked context words. Finally, new termhood estimations, referred to as *NC-values*, are calculated as a linear combination of the *C-values* and context factors for the respective terms. Evaluation of the *C/NC-methods* [3] has shown that contextual information improves term distribution in the extracted list by placing real terms closer to the top of the list.

3.2. Term variation management

Term variation and ambiguity are causing problems not only for ATR but for human experts as well. Several methods for term variation management have been developed. For example, the BLAST system [5] used approximate text string matching techniques and dictionaries to recognize spelling variations in gene and protein names. FASTR [6] handles morphological and syntactic variations by means of meta-rules used to describe term normalization, while semantic variants are handled via WordNet.

The basic *C-value* method has been enhanced by term variation management [2]. We consider a variety of sources from which term variation problems originate. In particular, we deal with orthographical, morphological, syntactic, lexico-semantic and pragmatic phenomena. Our approach to term variation management is based on term normalization as an integral part of the ATR process. Term variants (i.e. synonymous terms) are dealt with in the initial phase of ATR when term candidates are singled out, as opposed to other approaches (e.g. FASTR handles variants subsequently by applying transformation rules to extracted terms). Each term variant is normalized (see table 1 as an example) and term variants having the same normalized form are then grouped into classes in order to link each term candidate

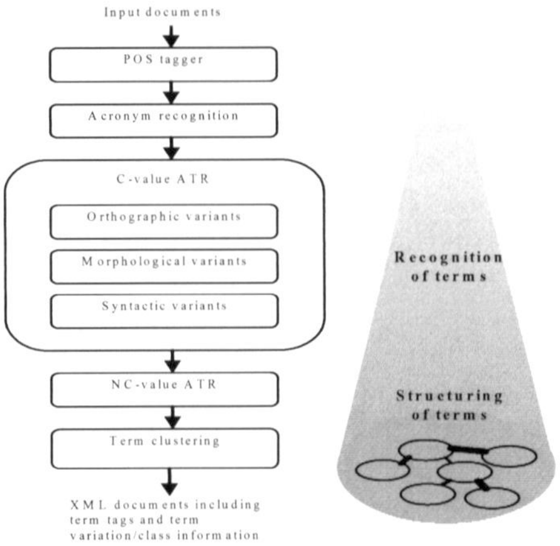

Figure 2: Ontology development

to all of its variants. This way, a list of normalized term candidate classes, rather than a list of single terms is statistically processed. The termhood is then calculated for a whole class of term variants, not for each term variant separately.

Table 1: Automatic term normalization

Term variants		Normalised term
human cancers	} →	human cancer
cancer in humans		
human's cancer		
human carcinoma		

3.3. Term clustering

Beside term recognition, term clustering is an indispensable component of the literature mining process. Since terminological opacity and polysemy are very common in molecular biology and biomedicine, term clustering is essential for the semantic integration of terms, the construction of domain ontologies and semantic tagging.

ATC in our system is performed using a hierarchical clustering method in which clusters are merged based on average mutual information measuring how strongly terms are related to one another [7]. Terms automatically recognized by the *NC-value* method and their co-occurrences are used as input, and a dendrogram of terms is produced as output. Parallel symmetric processing is used for high-speed clustering. The calculated term cluster information is encoded and used for calculating semantic similarities in SCE component. More precisely, the similarity between two individual terms is determined according to their position in a dendrogram. Also a commonality measure is defined as the number of shared ancestors between two terms in the dendrogram, and a positional measure as a sum of their distances from the root. Similarity between two terms corresponds to a ratio between commonality and positional measure.

Further details of the methods and their evaluations can be referred in [2,3].

4. Structuring knowledge

Literature mining can be regarded as a broader approach to IE/KA. IE and KA in our system are implemented through the integration of ATR, ATC, and ontology-based semantic similarity calculation. Graph-based visualization for globally structuring knowledge is also provided to facilitate KR and KA from documents. Additionally, the system supports combining different databases (papers and patents, technologies and innovations) and retrieves different types of knowledge simultaneously and crossly. This feature can accelerate knowledge discovery by combining existing knowledge. For example, discovering new knowledge on industrial innovation by structuring knowledge of trendy scientific paper database and past industrial innovation report database can be expected. Figure 3 shows an example of visualization of knowledge structures in the domain of innovation and engineering. In order to structure knowledge, the system draws a graph in which nodes indicate relevant KSs to keywords given and each links between KSs indicates semantic similarities dynamically calculated using ontology information developed by our ATR / ATC components. Since characterization for KSs using terminology is thought to be the most efficient and ultimate summarization to KSs, achieving a fast and just-in-time processing for structuring knowledge can be expected.

5. Conclusion

In this paper, we presented a system for literature mining and knowledge structuring over large KSs. The system is a terminology-based integrated KA system, in which we have integrated ATR, ATC, IR, similarity calculation, and visualization for structuring knowledge. It allows users to search and combine information from various sources. KA within the system is terminology-driven, with terminology information provided automatically. Similarity based knowledge retrieval is implemented through various semantic similarity calculations, which, in combination with hierarchical, ontology-based matching, offers powerful means for KA through visualization-based literature mining.

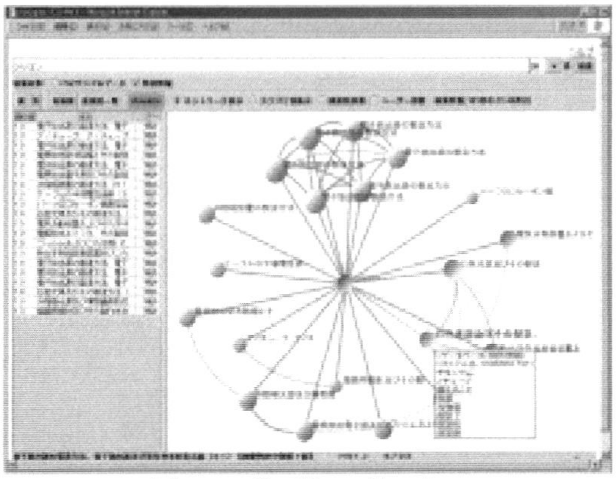

Figure 3: Visualization

Preliminary experiments we conducted show that the system's knowledge management scheme is an efficient methodology to facilitate KA and new knowledge discovery in the field of genome and nano-technology[2].

Important areas of future research will involve integration of a manually curated ontology with the results of automatically performed term clustering. Further, we will investigate the possibility of using a term classification system as an alternative structuring model for knowledge deduction and inference (instead of an ontology).

References

[1] K. Fukuda, T. Tsunoda, A. Tamura, T. Takagi, Toward information extraction: identifying protein names from biological papers, Proc. of PSB-98, Hawaii, 1998, pp. 3:705-716.

[2] H. Mima, S. Ananiadou, G. Nenadic, ATRACT workbench: an automatic term recognition and clustering of terms, in: V. Matoušek, P. Mautner, R. Mouček, K. Taušer (Eds.) Text, Speech and Dialogue, LNAI 2166, Springer Verlag, 2001, pp. 126-133.

[3] H. Mima, S. Ananiadou, An application and evaluation of the C/NC-value approach for the automatic term recognition of multi-word units in Japanese, Int. J. on Terminology 6/2 (2001), pp. 175-194.

[4] A. Voutilainen, J. Heikkila, An English Constraint Grammar (ENGCG) a surface-syntactic parser of English, in: U. Fries et al. (Eds.) Creating and Using English language corpora, Rodopi, Amsterdam, Atlanta, 1993, pp. 189-199.

[5] M. Krauthammer, A. Rzhetsky, P. Morozov, C. Friedman, Using BLAST for identifying gene and protein names in journal articles, in: Gene 259 (2000), pp. 245-252.

[6] C. Jacquemin, Spotting and discovering terms through NLP, MIT Press, Cambridge MA, 2001, p. 378.

[7] A. Ushioda, Hierarchical clustering of words, Proc. of COLING '96, Copenhagen, Denmark, 1996, pp. 1159-1162.

Determining the Specificity of Terms based on Information Theoretic Measures

Pum-Mo Ryu and Key-Sun Choi
Dept. EECS/KORTERM KAIST
373-1 Guseong-dong Yuseong-gu
305-701 Daejeon
Korea
pmryu@world.kaist.ac.kr, kschoi@world.kaist.ac.kr

Abstract

This paper introduces new specificity determining methods for terms based on information theoretic measures. The specificity of terms represents the quantity of domain specific information that is contained in the terms. Compositional and contextual information of terms are used in proposed methods. As the methods don't rely on domain dependent information, they can be applied to other domains without extra processes. Experiments showed very promising results with the precision 82.0% when applied to the terms in MeSH thesaurus.

1 Introduction

The specificity of terms represents the quantity of domain specific information contained in the terms. If a term has large quantity of domain specific information, the specificity of the term is high. The specificity of a term X is quantified to positive real number as equation (1).

$$Spec(X) \in R^{+} \tag{1}$$

The specificity is a kind of necessary condition for term hierarchy, *i.e.*, if X_1 is one of ancestors of X_2, then $Spec(X_1)$ is less than $Spec(X_2)$. Thus this condition can be applied to automatic construction or evaluation of term hierarchy. The specificity also can be applied to automatic term recognition.

Many domain specific terms are multiword terms. When domain specific concepts are represented as multiword terms, the terms are classified into two categories based on composition of unit words. In the first category, new terms are created by adding modifiers to existing terms. For example "*insulin-dependent diabetes mellitus*" was created by adding modifier "*insulin-dependent*" to its hypernym "*diabetes mellitus*" as in Table 1. In English, the specific level terms are very commonly compounds of the generic level term and some modifier (Croft, 2004). In this case, compositional information is important to get meaning of the terms. In the second category, new terms are independent of existing terms. For example, "*wolfram syndrome*" is semantically related to its ancestor terms as in Table 1. But it shares no common words with its ancestor terms. In this case, contextual information is important to get meaning of the terms.

Node Number	Terms
C18.452.297	diabetes mellitus
C18.452.297.267	insulin-dependent diabet es mellitus
C18.452.297.267.960	wolfram syndrome

Table 1 Subtree of MeSH[1] thesaurus. Node numbers represent hierarchical structure of terms

Contextual information has been mainly used to represent the meaning of terms in previous works. (Grefenstette, 1994) (Pereira, 1993) and (Sanderson, 1999) used contextual information to find hyponymy relation between terms. (Caraballo, 1999) also used contextual information to determine the specificity of nouns. Contrary, compositional information of terms has not been commonly discussed. We propose new specificity measuring methods based on both compositional and contextual information. The methods are formulated as information theory like measures.

This paper consists as follow; new specificity measuring methods are introduced in section 2, and the experiments and evaluation on the methods are discussed in section 3, finally conclusions are drawn in section 4.

2 Specificity Measuring Methods

In this section, we describe information theory like methods to measure the specificity of terms. Here, we call information theory *like* methods, because some probability values used in these methods are

[1] MeSH is available at http://www.nlm.nih.gov/mesh. MeSH 2003 was used in this research.

not real probability, rather they are relative weight of terms or words.

In information theory, when a low probability message occurs on channel output, the quantity of *surprise* is large, and the length of bits to represent the message becomes long. Thus the large quantity of information is gained by the message (Haykin, 1994). If we regard the terms in corpus as the messages of channel output, the information quantity of the terms can be measured using information theory. A set of target terms is defined as equation (2) for further explanation.

$$T = \{t_k \mid 1 \le k \le n\} \quad (2)$$

where t_k is a term. In next step, a discrete random variable X is defined as equation (3).

$$X = \{x_k \mid 1 \le k \le n\} \quad p(x_k) = \text{Prob}(X = x_k) \quad (3)$$

where x_k is an event of t_k is observed in corpus, $p(x_k)$ is the probability of x_k. The information quantity, $I(x_k)$, gained after observing x_k, is used as the specificity of t_k as equation (4).

$$Spec(t_k) \approx I(x_k) = -\log p(x_k) \quad (4)$$

By equation (4), we can measure the specificity of t_k, by estimating $p(x_k)$. We describe three estimating methods for $p(x_k)$ in following sections.

2.1 Compositional Information based Method (Method 1)

By compositionality, the meaning of a term can be strictly predicted from the meaning of the individual words (Manning, 1999). This method is divided into two steps: In the first step, the specificity of each word is measured independently. In the second step, the specificity of composite words is summed up. For detail description, we assume that t_k consists of one or more words as equation (5).

$$t_k = w_1 w_2 ... w_m \quad (5)$$

where w_i is *i*-th word in t_k. In next step, a discrete random variable Y is defined as equation (6).

$$Y = \{y_i \mid 1 \le i \le m\} \quad p(y_i) = \text{Prob}(Y = y_i) \quad (6)$$

where y_i is an event of w_i occurs in term t_k, $p(y_i)$ is the probability of y_i. Information quantity, $I(x_k)$, in equation (4) is redefined as equation (7) based on previous assumption.

$$I(x_k) = -\sum_{i=1}^{m} p(y_i) \log p(y_i) \quad (7)$$

where $I(x_k)$ is average information quantity of all words in t_k. In this mechanism, $p(y_i)$ of informative words should be smaller than that of non informative words. Two information sources, word frequency, tf.idf are used to estimate $p(y_i)$ independently.

We assume that if a term is composed of low frequency words, the term have large quantity of domain information. Because low frequency words appear in limited number of terms, they have high discriminating ability. On this assumption, $p(y_i)$ in equation (7) is estimated as relative frequency of w_i in corpus. In this estimation, $P(y_i)$ for low frequency words becomes small.

tf.idf is widely used term weighting scheme in information retrieval (Manning, 1999). We assume that if a term is composed of high tf.idf words, the term have domain specific information. On this assumption, $p(y_i)$ in equation (7) is estimated as equation (8).

$$p(y_i) \approx p_{MLE}(w_i) = 1 - \frac{tf \cdot idf(w_i)}{\sum_j tf \cdot idf(w_j)} \quad (8)$$

where $tf{\cdot}idf(w)$ is tf.idf value of w. In this equation, $p(y_i)$ of high tf.idf words becomes small.

If the modifier-head structure is known, the specificity of the term is calculated incrementally starting from head noun. In this manner, the specificity of the term is always larger than that of the head term. This result answers to the assumption that more specific term has higher specificity. We use simple nesting relations between terms to analyze modifier-head structure as follows (Frantzi, 2000):

Definition 1 If two terms X and Y are terms in same semantic category and X is nested in Y as W_1XW_2, then X is head term, and W_1 and W_2 are modifiers of X.

For example, because "*diabetes mellitus*" is nested in "*insulin dependent diabetes mellitus*" and two terms are all disease names, "*diabetes mellitus*" is head term and "*insulin dependent*" is modifier. The specificity of Y is measured as equation (9).

$$Spec(Y) = Spec(X) + \alpha \cdot Spec(W_1) + \beta \cdot Spec(W_2) \quad (9)$$

where $Spec(X)$, $Spec(W_1)$, and $Spec(W_2)$ are the specificity of X, W_1, W_2 respectively. α and β are weighting schemes for the specificity of modifiers. They are found by experimentally.

2.2 Contextual Information based Method (Method 2)

There are some problems that are hard to address using compositional information alone. Firstly, although two disease names, "*wolfram syndrome*" and "*insulin-dependent diabetes mellitus*", share many common features in semantic level, they don't share any common words in lexical level. In this case, it is unreasonable to compare two specificity values based on compositional information. Secondly, when several words are combined into one term, there are additional semantic components that are not predicted by unit words. For example, "*wolfram syndrome*" is a kind of "*diabetes mellitus*". We can not predict the meaning of "*diabetes mellitus*" from two separate words "*wolfram*" and "*syndrome*". Thus we use contextual information to address these problems.

General terms are frequently modified by other words in corpus. Because domain specific terms have sufficient information in themselves, they are rarely modified by other words, (Caraballo, 1999). Under this assumption, we use probability distribution of modifiers as contextual information. Collecting sufficient modifiers from given corpus is very important in this method. To this end, we use Conexor functional dependency parser (Conexor, 2004) to analyze the structure of sentences. Among many dependency functions defined in the parser, "*attr*" and "*mod*" functions are used to extract modifiers from analyzed structures. This method can be applied the terms that are modified by other words in corpus.

Entropy of modifiers for a term is defined as equation (10).

$$H_{mod}(t_k) = -\sum_i p(mod_i, t_k) \log p(mod_i, t_k) \quad (10)$$

where $p(mod_i, t_k)$ is the probability of mod_i modifies t_k and it is estimated as relative frequency of mod_i in all modifiers of t_k. The entropy calculated by equation (10) is the average information quantity of all (mod_i, t_k) pairs. Because domain specific terms have simple modifier distributions, the entropy of the terms is low. Therefore inversed entropy is assigned to $I(x_k)$ in equation (4) to make specific terms get large quantity of information.

$$I(x_k) \approx \max_{1 \le i \le n}(H_{mod}(t_i)) - H_{mod}(t_k) \quad (11)$$

where the first term of approximation is the maximum modifier entropy of all terms.

2.3 Hybrid Method (Method 3)

In this section, we describe hybrid method to overcome shortcomings of previous two methods. In this method the specificity is measured as equation (12).

$$I(x_k) \approx \frac{1}{\gamma(\frac{1}{I_{Cmp}(x_k)}) + (1-\gamma)(\frac{1}{I_{Ctx}(x_k)})} \quad (12)$$

where $I_{Cmp}(x_k)$ and $I_{Ctx}(x_k)$ are information quantity measured by method1 and method 2 respectively. They are normalized value between 0 and 1. $\gamma (0 \le \gamma \le 1)$ is weight of two values. If $\gamma = 0.5$, the equation is harmonic mean of two values. Therefore $I(x_k)$ becomes large when two values are equally large.

3 Experiments and Evaluation

In this section, we describe our experiments and evaluate proposed methods.

We select a subtree of MeSH thesaurus for the experiment. "*metabolic diseases(C18.452)*" node is root of the subtree, and the subtree consists of 436 disease names which are target terms for specificity measuring. We used MEDLINE [2] database corpus (170,000 abstracts, 20,000,000 words) to extract statistical information.

Each method was evaluated by two criteria, coverage and precision. Coverage is the fraction of the terms which have the specificity by given method. Method 2 gets relatively lower coverage than method 1, because method 2 can measure the specificity only when both the terms and their modifiers occur in corpus. Method 1 can measure the specificity whenever parts of composite words appear in corpus. Precision is the fraction of correct specificity relations values as equation (13).

$$p = \frac{\#\ of\ R(p,c)\ with\ correct\ specificity}{\#\ of\ all\ R(p,c)} \quad (13)$$

where $R(p,c)$ is a parent-child relation in MeSH thesaurus. If child term c has larger specificity than that of parent term p, then the relation is said to have correct specificity. We divided parent-child relations into two types. Relations where parent term is nested in child term are categorized as type I. Other relations are categorized as type II. There are 43 relations in type I and 393 relations in type II. The relations in type I always have correct specificity provided modifier-head information method described in section 2.1 is applied.

We tested prior experiment for 10 human subjects to find out the upper bound of precision. The subjects are all medical doctors of internal medicine, which is closely related division to "*metabolic diseases*". They were asked to identify parent-child relationship for given term pairs. The average precisions of type I and type II were 96.6% and 86.4% respectively. We set these values as upper bound of precision for suggested methods.

[2] MEDLINE is a database of biomedical articles serviced by National Library of Medicine, USA. (http://www.nlm.nih.gov)

Methods		Precision			Coverage
		Type I	Type II	Total	
Human subjects(Average)		96.6	86.4	87.4	
Term frequency		100.0	53.5	60.6	89.5
Term tf·idf		52.6	59.2	58.2	89.5
Compositional Information Method (Method 1)	Word Freq.	37.2	72.5	69.0	100.0
	Word Freq.+Structure (α=β=0.2)	100.0	72.8	75.5	100.0
	Word tf·idf	44.2	75.3	72.2	100.0
	Word tf·idf +Structure (α=β=0.2)	100.0	76.6	78.9	100.0
Contextual Information Method (Method 2) (mod cnt>1)		90.0	66.4	70.0	70.2
Hybrid Method (Method 3) (tf·idf + Struct, γ=0.8)		95.0	79.6	82.0	70.2

Table 2. Experimental results (%)

The specificity of terms was measured with method 1, method 2, and method 3 as Table 2. Two additional methods, based on term frequency and term tf.idf, were experimented to compare compositionality based methods and term based methods.

Method 1 showed better performance than term based methods. This result illustrate basic assumption of this paper that specific concepts are created by adding information to existing concepts, and new concepts are expressed as new terms by adding modifiers to existing terms. Word tf.idf based method showed better precision than word frequency based method. This result illustrate that tf.idf of words is more informative than frequency of words.

Method 3 showed the best precision, 82.0%, because the two methods interacted complementary. In hybrid method, the weight value $\gamma = 0.8$ indicates that compositional information is more informative than contextual information for the specificity of domain specific terms.

One reason of the errors is that the names of some internal nodes in MeSH thesaurus are category names rather disease names. For example, as "*acid-base imbalance (C18.452.076)*" is name of disease category, it doesn't occur as frequently as other real disease names. Other predictable reason is that we didn't consider various surface forms of same term. For example, although "*NIDDM*" is acronym of "*non insulin dependent diabetes mellitus*", the system counted two terms separately. Therefore the extracted statistics can't properly reflect semantic level information.

4 Conclusion

This paper proposed specificity measuring methods for terms based on information theory like measures using compositional and contextual information of terms. The methods are experimented on the terms in MeSH thesaurus. Hybrid method showed the best precision of 82.0%, because two methods complemented each other. As the proposed methods don't use domain dependent information, they can be adapted to other domains without extra processes.

In the future, we will modify the system to handle various term formations such as abbreviated form. Finally we will apply the proposed methods to the terms of other specific domains.

5 Acknowledgements

This work was supported in part by Ministry of Science & Technology, Ministry of Culture & Tourism of Korean government, and Korea Science & Engineering Foundation.

References

Caraballo, S. A., Charniak, E. 1999. *Determining the Specificity of Nouns from Text*. Proceedings of the Joint SIGDAT Conference on Empirical Methods in Natural Language Processing and Very Large Corpora

Conexor. 2004. *Conexor Functional Dependency Grammar Parser*. http://www.conexor.com

Croft, W. 2004. *Typology and Universals. 2nd ed.* Cambridge Textbooks in Linguistics, Cambridge Univ. Press

Frantzi, K., et. al. 2000. *Automatic recognition of multi-word terms: the C-value/NC-value method.* Journal of Digital Libraries, vol. 3, num. 2

Grefenstette, G. 1994. *Explorations in Automatic Thesaurus Discovery.* Kluwer Academic Publishers

Haykin, S. 1994. *Neural Network*. IEEE Press

Manning, C. D. and Schutze, H. 1999. *Foundations of Statistical Natural Language Processing*. The MIT Presss

Pereira, F., Tishby, N., and Lee, L. 1993. *Distributational clustering of English words.* Proceedings of ACL

Sanderson, M. 1999. *Deriving concept hierarchies from text*. Proceedings of ACM S1GIR

Construction of Grammar-Based Term Extraction Model for Japanese

Koichi Takeuchi
Okayama University
3-1-1, Tsushimanaka,
700-8530, Okayama,
Japan,
koichi@cl.it.okayama-u.ac.jp

Kyo Kageura
Teruo Koyama
National Institute of Informatics
2-1-2 Hitotsubashi, Chiyoda-ku
101-8430, Tokyo,
Japan,
kyo,t_koyama@nii.ac.jp

Béatrice Daille
IRIN - Universite de Nantes
2, rue de la Houssiniere, BP 92208
F44322, Nantes, Cedex 3,
France,
Beatrice.Daille@irin.univ-nantes.fr

Laurent Romary
LORIA
Campus Scientifique, B.P. 239,
54506, VANDOEUVRE-les-NANCY Cedex,
France,
Laurent.Romary@loria.fr

Abstract

In this paper we propose a grammar-based term extraction model for Japanese toward construction of multilingual term dictionary. The proposed approach evaluates termhood using morphological patterns of terms. Most of terms in Japanese consist of compound nouns or simple phrases, but detailed grammatical patterns for term extraction have not been constructed because of their complex compounding mechanisms. Applying detailed morphological investigation to Japanese compounding, we make sure their structures of word formation that can be comparable to those of Indo-European terms such as English and French.

1 Introduction

The difficulty of term extraction is how to evaluate termhood. Since the role of a term is to denote a specific concept in a domain, termhood should be evaluated by the following two sides: the first is the strength of unity that is called as unithood (Nakagawa, 2000) of element words as a term, and the second is the domain specialty of the word.

Most of previous approaches (see (Kageura and Koyama, 2000)) took the latter, but the former, i.e., unithood of a term, is very important because unithood is directly related to the mechanisms of creation of new concept by composing words, which should reflect the integrity of the new concept.

Recently some of term extraction work focus on the unithood of words. Nakagawa (2000) incorporated a statistical method, while Jacquemin (1996), Ananiadou (1994), Daille (2003) successfully applied detailed morpho-syntactic pattern-based approaches to evaluating unithood on term extraction of French and English.

We construct grammatical patterns for Japanese term extraction on the framework of ACABIT system (Daille, 2003) in order to make comparable morpho-syntactic grammar to the Indo-European languages such as English and French. Clarifying the comparable structure of terms enables us to have a basic framework of multilingual term dictionary and multilingual term extraction.

2 Grammatical Patterns

Grammatical patterns are defined by means of three features: unit of integration, grammatical category, and origin of a word. Unit of integration means a word formation class according to morphology. The smallest unit of integration in compounds and phrases is a morpheme. Grammatical category means grammatical function of morpheme like a part-of-speech. Origin of a word means a type of word that has a great influence to compounding rules in Japanese. There are two types of origins, which are a word originated in old Japanese **(OJ)** and a word imported from Chinese or other languages **(IM)**. Each group of words tends to connect the same group of words when it composes a compound noun.

2.1 Grammatical Categories

Grammatical categories are defined according to the functionality of connecting the other morphemes, therefore, the categories do not exactly correspond to conventional categories of grammar. The categories, however, are comparable to Daille's approach from the functional point of view.

⟨Noun⟩(OJ)(IM): This includes not only a nominal noun but also a deverbal noun,[1] an adjectival noun,[2] a number and a symbol. Morphemes in **Noun** can compose compounds without grammatical limitation.

⟨AdjStem⟩(IM): This denotes an adjectival stem whose function is to modify the next morpheme. The morphemes in **AdjStem** does not come to head in compound nouns or phrases because it is a stem.

⟨Prefix⟩(IM): This denotes a prefix in Japanese.

⟨Suffix⟩(IM): This denotes a nominal suffix that does not change the grammatical category of compounded word.

⟨AdjStemSuffix⟩(IM): This denotes a suffix that derives a stem of adjective. Because of this function, the morpheme in **AdjStemSuffix** takes two morphemes at the both sides in order to be a word.

⟨NomSuffix⟩(OJ): This denotes a suffix that derives a noun connecting to a stem of adjective, i.e., **AdjStemOJ** whose type is original Japanese (OJ).

⟨InfV⟩(OJ): This denotes a verb with inflection.

⟨InfA⟩(OJ): This denotes an adjective with inflection.

⟨AdjStemOJ⟩(OJ): This denotes a stem of adjective whose type is original Japanese. The morpheme **AdjStemOJ** needs to be followed by **NomSuffix** in order to be a word.

⟨ConOf⟩(OJ): This denotes a post positional particle whose function is to compose a phrase connecting two nouns. Roughly speaking, the grammatical function of the particle corresponds to 'of' in English.

[1]Deverbal noun has both characteristics of noun and verb. Basically, it acts as noun but it can be a verb followed by an auxiliary verb.

[2]Adjectival noun has both characteristics of noun and adjective.

2.2 Grammatical Patterns of Japanese terms

After we describe grammatical patterns of words as a stable unit, we show the patterns of compounds and phrases as a term based on the patterns of words.

Patterns of words are denoted as **WordIM** and **WordOJ** according to the types of origins of words. The patterns are described in Backus Naur Form (BNF).

$$\begin{aligned}&\langle WordIM\rangle\\ &::= \langle Noun\rangle|\langle AdjStem\rangle\langle Noun\rangle|\\ &\quad\langle Prefix\rangle\langle Noun\rangle|\langle Noun\rangle\langle Suffix\rangle|\\ &\quad\langle Noun\rangle\langle AdjStemSuffix\rangle\langle Noun\rangle|\\ &\quad\langle AdjStem\rangle\langle AdjStemSuffix\rangle\langle Noun\rangle|\\ &\quad\langle Prefix\rangle\langle Noun\rangle\langle Suffix\rangle\end{aligned}$$

$$\begin{aligned}&\langle WordOJ\rangle\\ &::= \langle InfV\rangle\langle Suffix\rangle|\\ &\quad\langle AdjStemOJ\rangle\langle NomSuffix\rangle|\\ &\quad\langle InfV\rangle\langle Noun\rangle|\langle InfV\rangle\langle SuffixV\rangle|\\ &\quad\langle InfA\rangle\langle Noun\rangle\end{aligned}$$

Patterns of compounds are also divided into two types that are related to **WordIM** and **WordOJ**, respectively. The former type of words **(IM)** can compose compounds without limitation because of their strong unithood, while the later words **OJ** can compose compounds within limited patterns. Since the restriction is not a grammatical theory but a kind of empirical knowledge.

$$\begin{aligned}\langle CompIM\rangle ::= &\ \langle CompIM\rangle\langle WordIM\rangle|\\ &\ \langle WordIM\rangle\langle CompIM\rangle|\\ &\ \langle WordIM\rangle\end{aligned}$$

$$\begin{aligned}\langle CompOJ\rangle ::= &\ \langle WordOJ\rangle|\\ &\ \langle InfA\rangle\langle NomSuffix\rangle\langle Noun+\rangle|\\ &\ \langle Noun\rangle\langle InfV\rangle\langle Suffix\rangle|\\ &\ \langle Noun\rangle\langle InfV\rangle\langle Noun\rangle\end{aligned}$$

Where $\langle Noun+\rangle$ means

$$\langle Noun+\rangle ::= \langle Noun\rangle|\langle Noun+\rangle\langle Noun\rangle$$

Patterns of terms consist of those of compounds and simple phrases. The grammatical patterns of simple phrases are limited to only "A no (of) B" since this pattern is the simplest phrase keeping unithood. Therefore grammatical patterns of terms we defined are as follows.

$$\langle Phrase \rangle ::= \langle CompIM \rangle \langle ConOF \rangle \langle CompIM \rangle$$
$$\langle TERM \rangle ::= \langle CompIM \rangle | \langle CompOJ \rangle | \langle Phrase \rangle$$

3 Preliminary Experiment

We made two types of experiments for Japanese ACABIT system. The first evaluation is about the coverage of morphological patterns. We input technical terms to Japanese ACABIT and check the rate of acceptability of the patterns. The second experiment is term extraction performance. For this experiment, we use the set of abstracts and author's keywords distributed by NII(Kageura et al., 2000).

3.1 Overview of ACABIT system

Japanese ACABIT system detects nominal expressions by local grammar rules we elaborated in Section 2.[3] Since the input of ACABIT needs POS tagged information, we apply Japanese morphological analyzer ChaSen (Matsumoto et al., 1999). The output of ACABIT is a list of two-words candidate terms ranked according to the degree of representativeness of the corpus using the log-likelihood statistics (Dunning, 1993).

3.2 Coverage of patterns

We prepare three kinds of technical terms: 1) a technical term dictionary of information processing (ipdic), 2) a term dictionary in computer domain (comdic) and 3) a list of author's keywords in artificial intelligence domain (jsai) (Kageura and Koyama, 2000).[4] All terms are analyzed by ChaSen first. After this process, we evaluate quantitative nature of terms about number of one word terms and number of phrasal terms

Table 1 shows that the ratio of one word term is not small, i.e., more than 10% for every source. So the upper bounds for extracting complex terms are 86.4% (ipdic), 88.4% (comdic) and 84.4% (jsai). Table 2 shows the results of coverage performance of Japanese ACABIT.

[3]One morpheme pattern such as **Noun** in our grammatical category is deleted in this application because one morpheme pattern is too noisy to detect terms.

[4]It is abstracts of Japanese society of artificial intelligence.

Table 1: Statistics of input terms

	One word terms (%)	phrasal terms (%)
ipdic	2207/16275(13.6)	409/16275(2.5)
comdic	4480/38785(11.6)	2366/38785 (6.1)
jsai	658/4206(15.6)	231/4206(5.5)

Table 2: Coverage of Japanese ACABIT

	coverage (%)
ipdic	12195/16275(74.9)
comdic	28162/38785(72.6)
jsai	3056/4206(72.7)

ACABIT works well. The upper bound of this experiment is about from 86% to 89% for these terms. The error types are categorized into two: Variety of term: most errors occur for terms that contain proper nouns. For example, "nyuuton" (Newton) in "nyutonn hou" (Newton method) is annotated proper noun in ChaSen. We just excluded this sort of patterns as they are unlikely to make terms. Errors of annotation of ChaSen: ChaSen makes annotation errors on ambiguous words.

3.3 Keyword extraction

Japanese ACABIT is applied to abstracts in the domain of artificial intelligence in order to show term extraction performance. Assuming that author's keywords are correct terms, we evaluate the performance of ACABIT by comparing extracted terms with author's keywords. Table 3 shows the statistics of author's keywords. According to the table, 68.7% the keywords occur in the abstracts of which 20.1% are one-word keywords. So 2308 words are the upper bound for the extraction experiment.

Table 3: Statistics of author's keywords

	author's keywords (%)
contained in text	2890/4206 (68.7)
one word keyword	582/2890 (20.1)
upper bound	2308/4206 (54.9)

Table 4 shows the results of term extraction comparison to author's keywords. We evaluate precision, and correct rate to upper bound of author's keywords.

All extracted terms are evaluated. In Table 4, ACABIT works well because 71% to upper bound are successfully extracted. The precision

Table 4: Results of term extraction

	author's keywords (%)
precision	1639/ 23494(7.0)
recall to upper bound	1639/2308(71.0)

is, however, poor. When we filter out the candidates with low log-likelihood value terms, precision becomes 20.8% (and recall with respect to upper bound was 25.0%). Example correctly extracted words are "iden-teki-arugorizumu" (generic algorithm), "chishiki-beisu" (knowledge base), and wrong examples are "honronbun" (this paper), "hon-kenkyu" (this research) "hissya-ra" (authors). The words that are extracted wrongly are high frequency words in target text.

4 Discussions

Comparing with the results of French term extraction (Jacqumin et al. 2002) using ACABIT system, termhood precision and recall are 79% and 67.5% in French (Daille, 1996), respectively. A precision in English is 67% (Savary, 2001). The recall rate of Japanese ACABIT is almost the same as the results in French, thus, we can conclude the proposed morpho-syntactic patterns have good coverage for technical terms. The precision of keyword extraction is poor, however, it is not the current target since the proposed approach is intended to evaluate unithood of terms without domain dependence.

The current approach does not extract uniterms that account for a fifth in keywords (Table 3) since uniterms have naturally strong unithood and the proposed approach should not be applied to them. The problems of uniterms and low precision should be solved by investigating approaches how to evaluate specificity of words in a domain.

5 Conclusions

We proposed a pattern-based term extraction method and showed the experimental results. We tried to extract terms focusing on the unity of intra-term structure by morpho-syntactic patterns without domain dependence. From the experimental results, the constructed patterns worked well for coverage. This means that the proposed morpho-syntactic set is enough to be applied to a basic framework to describe grammatical structure of multilingual terms.

So far, we have only discussed the intra-structure of terms at the level of morpho-syntactic patterns of terms. To develop a multilingual term extraction model we need to delve further into two sides: The first is structural analyses of terms in sentences to evaluate specificity of words in a domain. The second is the multilingual correspondence between the terms at the level of individual correspondences of lexical items and POS-categories.

References

S. Ananiadou. 1994. A methodology for automatic term recognition. In *In Proceedings of the 15th International Conference on Computational Linguistics (COLING)*, pages 1034–1038.

Beatrice Daille. 1996. Study and implementation of combined techniques for automatic extraction of terminology. In *The Balancing Act: Combining Symbolic and Statistical Aplication to Language*, pages 49–66.

B. Daille. 2003. Terminology Mining. In M.T. Pazienza, editor, *Information Extraction in the Web Ea*, pages 29–44. Springer.

T. Dunning. 1993. Accurate methods for the statistics of surprise and coincidence. *Computational Linguistics*, 19(1):61–76.

C. Jacquemin. 1996. A symbolic and surgical acquisition of terms through variation. In E. Riloff S. Wermter and G. Scheler (Eds.), editors, *In Connectionist, Statistical and Symbolic Approaches to Learning for Natural Language Processing.*

K. Kageura and T. Koyama. 2000. *Terminology, vol.6 no.2.* John Benjamins Publishing Company.

K. Kageura, M. Yoshioka, and T. Koyama. 2000. Towards a common testbed for corpus-based terminology: Lexical units, POS information and their utilisation. In *First International Symposium on Advanced Informatics (AdInfo2000).*

Y. Matsumoto, A. Kitauchi, T. Yamashita, and Y. Hirano, 1999. *Japanese Morphological Analysis System ChaSen 2.0 Users Manual.*

H. Nakagawa. 2000. Automatic term recognition based on statistics of compound nouns. *Terminology*, 6(2):195–210.

A. Savary. 2001. Etude comparative de deux outils d'acquisition de termes complexes. In *In TIA-2001 (4th meeting Terminology and Artificial Intelligence).*

Author Index

Association for Computational Linguistics
209 N. Eighth Street
Stroudsburg, Pennsylvania 18360

CURRAN ASSOCIATES INC
proceedings
.com

Asphalt Mixtures and Materials 2018

Transportation Research Record: Journal of the Transportation Research Board

Volume 2672, Issue 28

SAGE Publishing